Message of Bhagavad Gita

(In 126 Chosen Shlokas)

Part 1: TVAM - Your Higher SELF

Transcribed and Edited by Atmajyotis
(Based on Sri Prabhuji's Satsangs)

An offering from
LIGHT OF THE SELF FOUNDATION

Dedication

Many Atmajyotis have worked selflessly to transcribe
and publish this book based on talks of
Sadguru Sri Prabhuji.

With deep love and respect we dedicate this book to
all Atmajyotis. May this effort of all Atmajyotis reach
spiritual seekers all over the world, with this intention,
we release this book.

lokāha samasthāha sukhino bhavantu

Gita Jayanthi, December 2022

TABLE OF CONTENTS

FOREWORD

Srimad Bhagavad Gita is the sacred teaching of Sri Krishna. During the Mahabharata war, Arjuna's mind was full of anxiety and sorrow; he was confused between Dharma and Adharma. Bhagavad Gita is the teaching of Sri Krishna to the confused and depressed Arjuna. He was shown the path of Dharma by the supreme grace of the Lord.

Bhagavad Gita however isn't just a message delivered to Arjuna alone, it is the universal message given by the Vishwa Guru Sri Krishna to the entire human race. Arjuna was just an instrument. It is a sacred teaching for each and every one of us. What is the teaching? The Gita gives us the wisdom to attain liberation. It is a sacred scripture that shows us the path to *mukti* and uplifts us.

What do we have to do for that? ***ātmano mokshārtam jagad hitayacha*** - (Self Realization and Social Service) should be the mantra of our life. Hence the main teaching of Sri Krishna in Bhagavad Gita is *Brahma Vidya* (Knowledge of the Absolute) and *Yoga Shastra* (Yogic Science). Once we realize that the individual self and the supreme Self are one and the same, we attain *moksha*, we are liberated. Hence Sri Krishna teaches the truth of the inner self through Brahma Vidya, the knowledge that helps us merge with the supreme Self, *Paramātma*. To attain this knowledge, *brahmajnāna*, the mind should be purified. Hence Sri Krishna teaches us *Yoga Shastra* - how to lead an ethical and moral life and walk on the path of Dharma. This alone helps us to purify our minds.

yatra yogeśhvaraḥ kṛiṣhṇo
yatra pārtho dhanur-dharaḥ
tatra srir vijayo bhūtir
dhruvā nītir matir mama

Wherever there is Sri Krishna, the Lord of all Yoga, and wherever there is Arjuna, the supreme archer, there will also certainly be unending opulence, victory, prosperity, and righteousness. Of this, I am certain.

This sloka highlights the supreme importance of studying the Gita. Just like Arjuna, we should all become disciples of Sri Krishna. The teaching of Gita should be implemented in our day-to-day life. Only then 'Sri', meaning success in material life and 'Vijaya', meaning success in spiritual life will be obtained. This is the most important verse told by Sri Krishna in the last verse of the last chapter of the Bhagavad Gita (BG 18.78). The ones who study and implement Bhagavad Gita in their day-to-day life and teach this supreme knowledge to others are the closest and most lovable to God. Is there anything more important in life than being close to God?

Atmajyoti Satsang's Gita Jyoti Study Circles have many volunteers who are doing selfless service. The acharyas and acharyanis of the Study Circles are involved in various activities like teaching Bhagavad Gita verses, explaining their meaning, giving discourses, and generally spreading the message of the Gita to the world. They are an inspiration to many people. This seva is sure to bring a lot of good merit to all, because this activity is most lovable to God.

With the intention of passing the message of Bhagavad Gita in a simplified manner, 126 slokas from the 18 chapters have been carefully selected and summarized into a book. There are many Atmajyotis who have put in efforts to preserve my teachings and transcribe them into a book which is understandable to one and all. May the Supreme Lord bless them and their families. May their efforts be fruitful. May the light and wisdom of Gita flow into the lives of many more and uplift the entire world.

Sri Prabhuji
December 2022

PREFACE

The Bhagavad Gita is the song sung by the Lord. Listening to the Bhagavad Gita, chanting its verses and spreading the knowledge of Bhagavad Gita is considered very noble work.

Of all the *yajnas* and *pujas* that we offer to the Almighty, offering or spreading the wisdom of the scriptures is the greatest and noblest of all. All forms of worship give us good merit, but the greatest merit is gained by *jnāna yajna*, the service of spreading the Lord's message to the world.

Bhagavad Gita is a spiritual scripture. The path of spirituality shows us the divinity within. We look for God everywhere; we go to temples and undertake pilgrimage. But salvation lies only in realizing our own divinity. Bhagavad Gita is the Song of the Lord Himself, the ultimate truth imparted by Bhagavān Sri Krishna to Arjuna. Thus one who wishes to reach the ultimate reality has to necessarily study the Gita.

The Gita is the essence of all our scriptures - the Upanishads and the Vedas. Vedas are four in number - *rig, yajur, sāma and atharvana*. They begin with *karmakānda* and end with *jnānakānda*. In the *jnānakānda*, the portion which explains the meaning and essence of Vedas is called Upanishad.

Upanishad consists of the essence of all the Vedas. There are several Upanishads, 108 or even more. Out of these, the three great acharyas - Shankara, Madhva and Ramanuja have written the abstract or *bhashya* for ten important Upanishads.

The Upanishads contain the revelations of our ancient sages about the truth of existence - which is 'I am in the divine and the divine is in me'. The study of the Upanishads is also a *jnāna yajna*. The essence of the Upanishads is narrated by Sri Krishna to Arjuna in the Bhagavad Gita. Therefore if we study the Gita, the truth realized by the great rishis will be realized by us as well.

The realization of this Truth is called Jnāna. Jnāna destroys *ajnāna* - that about which we are ignorant. What is it that we do not know? We know everything about the outer world, like how to be a businessman, an engineer, how to cook etc. But what we do not know is, 'Who am I?' We assume that 'I' refers to the body, man or woman. We can go only as far as the body, mind and intellect and we think this is 'I'.

The Bhagavad Gita eliminates this ignorance about our identity with body, mind and intellect. It reveals that they are only the instruments or vehicles through which we operate!

Says Bhagavān, your mind, body and intellect are also vehicles, just as a car, bus or airplane is. You are the passenger, the *jivātma* who inhabits the body, mind and intellect. You are the Paramātma, the energy driving this vehicle. *mukti* or liberation is when you, the *jiva* realizes 'I am not this body, mind and intellect, I am one in the divine, I am *ātmaswaroopi*. So the essence of Bhagavad Gita is,

nānu, nānembudu nānalla
ee deha mana buddhi nānalla
sachchidānandātma shiva nānu nāne
shivoham shivoham shivoham

I am not what I think I am, I am not this body and mind or intellect; I am pure consciousness, Shivoham, Shivoham, Shivoham.

Over several lifetimes, we would've experienced a lot of good and bad things, accumulated merits and demerits. To experience and exhaust the results of these good-bad results, we have to be reborn yet again and again, *punarapi maranam, punarapi jananam, punarapi janani jatare shayanam,* sings Adi Shankaracharya; we are compelled to go through the repeated cycles of birth and death, and thus we end up in the mother's womb again and again.

With every new birth comes *ajnāna*, ignorance. With ignorance comes *pāpa-punya*, merit and demerit, which keep accumulating. This treasure-chest of endless *pāpa-punya* can be emptied only by diving into the *jnāna* of Bhagavad Gita.

"Can I let only the demerits go, and hang on to the merits?" is the clever question asked by the mind! But, says Krishna, both *pāpa-punya*, good-bad should go, because both are shackles that bind us. pāpa is the iron shackle and *punya* is the golden shackle, and we do not know which one binds us in what manner, both will certainly bind us to birth and death. Releasing ourselves from this bondage by realizing that "I am divine' is the message of Bhagavad Gita.

Right now, we operate in the world assuming, boasting that 'I am everything! There is no God! I am God!' The exact opposite of this is Self Realization - 'God is everything, There is nothing called I, I implies the ego'. When this realization happens, this is called *ātma jnāna, advaita jnāna.* We should study Bhagavad Gita for this *advaita jnāna*, the knowledge of liberation. There are 18 chapters in the Bhagavad Gita. It can be classified into three groups of six chapters each. In the first six chapters, the Lord explains who we are. In the next 6 chapters, He reveals about Himself, that is Ishwara, the creator. In the last six chapters, that is from 13th to 18th chapters, He explains about our relationship with God. Thus the Bhagavad Gita is the essence of the mahavākya of Upanishads - *tat tvam asi* - You Are That.

tat means 'Ishwara', **tvam** means 'you', **asi** means 'you are Ishwara', which means you are the form of Ishwara. We may feel "oh no, how is this possible? how can I be the form of God, this is not acceptable, this is thought is sin, this is injustice". This happens because we mistake the I for the Ego. When we stop identifying with the Ego, the real 'I' is revealed, we will realize 'I am Ishwara'. That is liberation, taught in the Bhagavad Gita.

ātma darshanam brahma darshanam
brahma darshanam satya darshanam

First and foremost we need to investigate, understand and become aware of what or who is this 'I'. This is called *ātma darshana*. Once we are aware about who we are, then the awareness of God will happen. This is called *brahma darshana*. Realizing that *ātma* and *brahma* are the same is *satya darshana*. This is the ultimate truth and everything else is a lie, a dream, an illusion - *māya*. The Bhagavad Gita leads us out of this illusion.

So, what is the subject matter of the Bhagavad Gita? Essentially, the Gita talks about two things - Jnāna (knowledge) and Karma (action). What kind of Jnāna? *ātmajnāna*; who am I, what is my relationship with God? What is Karma? How to lead life, how to perform action, how to purify my heart and attain liberation - this is called *karma mārga*, the Path of Karma. *ātmajnāna* implies *brahmajnāna*. Karma tells the way to lead our life. Understand these two and you will be liberated, says Lord Krishna.

No other scripture in the entire world teaches the means of liberation with such clarity and simplicity. The Gita has more than 700 verses. It might not be possible for most of us to study all the 700-plus verses; hence this effort of distilling the essence of the Bhagavad Gita in 126 selected verses. The summary of these 126 verses have been further divided into three parts and published as three separate books; hence we need to read all the three books to get the entire essence of the Gita.

This book has the summary of chapters 1 to 6, explained with the selected verses, and published as MESSAGE OF BHAGAVAD GITA Part 1: Tvam - Your Higher Self.

- **Sri Prabhuji**

CHAPTER 1: ARJUNA VISHĀDA YOGA

Introduction

My pranāms to all the Atmajyotis, Divine Light of the Self.

Today we have gathered here to conduct this Gita Jnāna Yajna. *yajna* is an offering for the divine. Gita Jnāna Yajna is the highest form of offering sacrifice to the divine. We undertake many types of pujas and *yajnas*, many types of good activities, but whether it is *yajna* (fire-ritual), *dāna* (charity) or *puja* (worship), the highest form of *yajna* is Jnāna Yajna. *yajna* is a purification process, an offering, a sacrifice. For getting anything in life you have to offer something - suppose a boy wants to get good marks in an examination he has to offer his time, he has to sacrifice his time.

Similarly if you have to attain the highest supreme reality God in your life, you need to offer something. You have to offer your small nature, your ego in the fire of Jnāna for attaining the supreme reality. That is why this *yajna* is the most auspicious. It brings auspiciousness to all those who are participating in the *yajna*.

What is Gita Jnāna Yajna? Bhagavad Gita is the teaching of Sri Krishna Bhagavān. Bhagavad Gita is a part of the epic called Mahabharata. Mahabharata as you know is the story of Pandavas and Kauravas fighting for power, and also a war for establishing Dharma or righteousness. The epic, written by Vedavyasa Maharshi has over one lakh shlokas. Bhagavad Gita is a small text within the Mahabharata.

The theme of Mahabharata is the play of human egos, the play of different characters. It has a variety of characters; someone is seeking power, someone is fighting for power, someone is fighting for justice, someone is fighting for righteousness, someone is wise, someone is cunning... the play of all these characters is called Mahabharata. These characters can be found in our day to day life, in our own life, in people around us, in society. It is a psycho-drama, a mega epic. In a sense Mahabharata represents human society in totality. So why did Vyasa Maharshi write Mahabharata and insert the Bhagavad Gita?

Vyasa Maharshi wanted to tell us that despite all the melodrama of human life at the psychological plane, there is a possibility of upliftment, there is a way we can attain a higher consciousness. Bhagavad Gita, the summary of the teachings of all Upanishads, gives us this knowledge.

We know so many things in life; we know engineering, mathematics, physics, chemistry, etc. But there is one thing which we don't know, that is about ourselves. What we can know is only second hand information, based on how others perceive us. We don't have direct knowledge of our own selves, we are ignorant of our true nature. By studying the Gita, ignorance goes and truth shines, the truth that 'I am not the body, mind or intellect but I am pure consciousness'. Pure consciousness is God.

The second aspect of teaching of Bhagavad Gita is Karma. For attaining *brahmajnāna*, we need to purify our mind, we need to be true in our actions. This purification is required before we can acquire the knowledge of the Self. Bhagavad Gita purifies us by the teaching of Karma Yoga - how to perform actions in our life.

May all of us understand the message of Bhagavad Gita and participate in this Jnāna Yajna, purify ourselves through Karma Yoga and attain the Brahma Vidya, Supreme Knowledge. May all of us become free from all karmic impressions and attain the highest goals of spiritual life - *ātmajnāna*, *mukti*. May all of us be liberated in this life and become Jivanmuktas.

****

Shloka 1.1

Dhritarashtra said: O Sanjaya, after gathering on the holy field of Kurukshetra, and desiring to fight, what did my sons and the sons of Pandu do?

Let us contemplate on the first chapter first shloka of the Bhagavad Gita. The first chapter of the Gita is titled Arjuna Vishāda Yoga. Arjuna Vishāda means depression of Arjuna. You will be happy to know, Arjuna also felt depressed! Depression is not a new disease, it was there a few thousand years ago also!

Why did Arjuna get depressed? Arjuna came to the war, the Mahabharata war and he saw his opponents were his own Gurus, his own teachers, his own relatives, his grandfather…killing all these people he felt would incur sin, and this caused depression in him, this is the first chapter. The first chapter opens with a conversation between Dhritarashtra and Sanjaya. Dhritarashtra is a blind king who has a hundred children- they are called Kauravas. Dhritarashtra has a charioteer, Sanjaya. In Dharmakshetra, the Kurukshetra, warriors have gathered. What are my people doing and Pandavas doing…the chapter opens with Dharma-kshetra Kuru-kshetra. Kshetra means field, like an agriculture field. What do you mean by field? You sow something and you reap something. If you sow mango you will get mango fruits. If you sow karela (bitter gourd) you will get karela fruit. So whatever you sow, you will reap. Likewise, we operate in a field, in a space where we can sow either Dharma, seeds of Dharma or seeds of Karma. If you sow seeds of Dharma, you get fruits of Dharma. If you sow seeds of Karma you will get fruits of Karma. So that is why the chapter appropriately starts withDharma-*kshetre kuru-kshetre…*

dharmakshetra means a place where dharmic actions are done. *kurukshetra* means the field belonging to Kauravas, and Kauravas were the ones who played politics, played for selfish reasons and kept on harassing the Pandavas. So Kauravas represent karmic impressions. The Mahabharata war is a field where Dharma and Karma play out. Thus it is not only in this Mahabharata war, in our life too it's the same. We can convert our life to a field of Dharma or a field of Karma. What is the field of Dharma? What is Dharma altogether?

Dharma is not religion. Dharma is the fundamental principle of the universe, the fundamental structure of the universe. Everything in the universe has an order… stars, planets and galaxies move with a specific order. There is no chaos, there is no accident. Similarly atoms, molecules, electrons and subatomic particles operate with a certain principle, within a certain structure. Even though things are constantly moving there is a structure in the movement, there is an order in the movement, there is no chaos. This order is called Dharma. There is an order in you also - the heart is beating, your eyes are operating, your ears are operating, the brain is working, all these are structured operations, right? There is what you call a law in the universe which is maintaining this order. So whatever action you do, if it is in tune with Dharma, in tune with order, it becomes a dharmic action. If you are not in tune with Dharma it becomes karmic action.

The first shloka is very relevant to us. In our lives, are we performing dharmic actions or karmic actions which are selfishly oriented? Then the name Dhritarashtra; 'Dhrita' means 'to hold', 'Rashtra' means kingdom; so one who is holding his Kingdom tightly is Dhritarashtra… sounds very familiar right? Many of our politicians hold their chairs so tightly! They are not even ready to give it to their children. But Dhritarashtra is holding the Kingdom to give it to his children. Here he has a tight hold on the Kingdom, that is why he is called Dhritarashtra. He doesn't want to give to anybody else, it has to go only to his children. And he is blind. When I say blind, there is a physical blindness, sure - he is not to see anybody. But there is a psychological blindness or spiritual blindness too where he is not able to understand what is right and what is wrong, what is Dharma and what is *adharma*. He is not able to see how his children are going wrong, behaving in an adharmic manner. He is not able to see that - this is psychological or spiritual blindness. Thus Dhritarashtra represents both physical blindness and spiritual blindness.

Sanjaya means victory. It is quite the opposite of Dhritarashtra. Dhritarashtra is not able to see, Sanjaya is able to see. Sanjaya is able to see not only what is in front of him, he is able to see beyond too. He is able to sit in the palace and see the Mahabharata war. He had a divine vision granted by Sri Veda Vyasa Maharshi and so Sanjaya had the good fortune of receiving the teachings of Sri Krishna. Other than Arjuna, Sanjaya is the only person who received the teaching of Sri Krishna directly. Other than Arjuna it was Sanjaya who had the cosmic vision, saw the cosmic form of the Lord. Thus Sanjaya is the fortunate and victorious one.

This conversation is happening between the blind king and wise charioteer. The king addresses the two sides as - māmakāḥ - my children, and pāṇḍavāḥ - children of Pandu. The children of Pandu are also related to him, they are his brother's children, but he distinguishes between them. He is more focused on his children and is eager to know what they are upto.

In a sense, this shloka is telling us to look at our own lives, our actions, our fields of actions. Are we converting our field of action into Dharmakshetra or Kurukshetra? Are we living the life of the blind king or of Sanjaya, the wise man? This blind king is holding on to his kingdom, he is attached to the kingdom, and all attachment leads to misery.

At the end of the war when all the hundred children of Dhritarashtra are killed, he cries in front of Sri Krishna - what sin have I committed for facing this misfortune? Sri Krishna said, 50 lifetimes ago you had killed hundred siblings of birds, the parents of birds cursed you so that you may also have the same suffering, arising out of the death of your children. Dhritarashtra starts crying louder - why did I have to wait for 50 lifetimes to suffer this misfortune? Sri Krishna says - to acquire 100 children you needed to acquire the merit over 50 lifetimes, and at the end of it all they had to be killed because of the sin you have committed 50 lifetimes ago. This is the way Karma plays out. The results of Karma cannot be judged, because it is a set of cumulative actions over many lifetimes. Anything happening in our life is a karmic play, good or bad. So accept life as it comes and perform your actions in a dharmic way. This is the message of the first shloka of the Bhagavad Gita.

To sum up, our life can be a field of Dharma or a field of Karma. Karma means selfish actions. The more and more selfish actions we get involved in, we accumulate more and more karmic impressions, we have to undergo more and more cycles of birth and death. To be free from the cycle of birth and death, we have to make our life a field of Dharma.

dhṛitarāśhtra uvācha,
dharma-kṣhetre kuru-kṣhetre samavetā yuyutsavaḥ I
māmakāḥ pāṇḍavāśhchaiva kimakurvata sañjaya
II 1.1 II

****

CHAPTER 2: SĀNKHYA YOGA

Shloka 2.7

I am confused about my duty, and am besieged with anxiety and faintheartedness. I am Your disciple, and am surrendered to You. Please instruct me for certain what is best for me

The second chapter of the Bhagavad Gita is titled Sānkhya Yoga. Sānkhya also means Jnāna, wisdom. Sānkhya also means *sanyāsa*, renunciation. Wisdom is knowledge of the Self. *sanyāsa* means 'to drop'. But, not dropping friends, family, job etc. Renouncing ignorance is called *sanyāsa*. The literal meaning of *sanyāsa* is *samyak-nyasa. nyasa* means 'deposit', *samyak* means 'appropriate'. *samyak-nyasa* means the right kind of deposit. Your mind should renounce ignorance and be deposited in knowledge - that is called *sanyāsa*. What is knowledge about the Self?

nānu nānembudu nānalla,
ee deha mana buddhi nānalla,
sachchidānanda ātma shiva nānu nāne,
shivoham shivoham shivoham

I am not what I think I am, I am not the body, mind, or intellect, I am Pure Consciousness, I am Shiva

The right knowledge is I am not the body, I am not the mind, I am not the intellect; I am pure consciousness, I am of the nature of divinity, I am one with Supreme reality Brahman. This is Brahmavidya. Brahmavidya has two parts; one is understanding who I am- Jnāna, and dropping what I am not - Sanyasa. so this is the essence of *Sānkhya Yoga.*

In this verse, Arjuna out of his depression tries to find what is right and what is wrong, what is Dharma and what is Adharma. He is not able to comprehend what is right, his mind is deluded, clouded. Arjuna's mind is clouded seeing his relatives and friends lined up on the battlefield. He has to kill them and he thinks it is a sin. But as a warrior his duty is to fight for righteousness- Dharma. If he doesn't fight he will be failing in his duty. If he fights he will be killing his relatives so he is in a dilemma. Even though Arjuna had fought many wars and won, this is the mother of all wars, and cowardliness has gripped him, attachment has gripped him. Wherever there's attachment, there is always suffering. A judge known for impartiality and punishes every criminal rightfully, but if it's his son standing in front of him one day as a criminal, he will not be able to give the right judgment; his sense of duty will clouded, he will not be able to punish his son with ease because he is attached to him. The same happened with a doctor - a renowned heart surgeon - he had operated on hundreds and thousands of patients. He had never failed, until his mother was wheeled in one day in an emergency situation, she had a heart attack. The doctor's hand shakes while performing the surgery, and he fails. He is attached to his mother.

Arjuna faced the same situation, but fortunately for him, he was able to see that his mind was clouded, he was not able to think, and sought help. But most of us don't even realize that we need help. Even in that clouded condition we think we are right. Intelligence is required to understand that 'I am in a mess'. Else we keep struggling in that mess, thinking we are on the right track. So to seek help some intelligence is required. Arjuna says to Krishna, "O' Krishna, cowardice has gripped me, I am not able to understand what is right and what is wrong, can you please guide me? Please show me the way, I have become your disciple".

This verse also tells us that we need to seek help from someone who can help, who can guide us properly. Arjuna of course knew Sri Krishna as God Himself but had never thought of him as guru or teacher. He orders Sri Krishna as his charioteer. He treats him like a driver but once he releases that he is lost he is on his knees, begging Sri Krishna to show him the way. In a way this is our situation as well; we know that God is great, all powerful, but we treat God like a charioteer, a driver. Our prayers are selfish - O' God my child is going for an examination, she didn't study well, please make sure she gets 100 marks', 'O! God I need some money , bless me'... we also treat god like a charioteer.

Only when we realize that somebody who is in a higher position, a position of authority, or has a greater wisdom than us, we approach that person as a Guru. We will not become disciples immediately even then; we think we know and keep struggling, but when we understand that there is something beyond our understanding, we need to seek help, approach the Guru. Unless you approach a Guru by yourself, the Guru will not teach. The Guru is a teacher of wisdom, of enlightenment, of Mukti - liberation. When you approach the Guru with the attitude of surrender, he will start teaching. Now Arjuna has surrendered and he prays to Krishna - please show me the way. So Krishna starts teaching now.

karpanya-dosopahata-svabhavah
prcchami tvam dharma-sammudha-cetah
yac chreyah syan niscitam bruhi tan me
sisyas te 'ham sadhi mam tvam prapannam ||2.7||

Shloka 2.11

The Supreme Lord said: While you speak words of wisdom, you are mourning for that which is not worthy of grief. The wise lament neither for the living nor for the dead

The second chapter is titled Sānkhya Yoga. Sānkhya Yoga means the Yoga of knowledge. If you recollect in earlier verse, Arjuna gets depressed, worried and surrenders to Sri Krishna. He says, 'I am not able to fight the war in which my opponents are my relatives, my grandfathers, my gurus. I am your disciple, please show me the right path'. Sri Krishna could have very well said, Arjuna it's not ok for you to fight now, let's go, but instead Sri Krishna addresses the root problem of his grief.

Sri Krishna says, O' Arjuna, you are behaving like a learned man- *prajñā-vādān* - you are worrying, you are actually getting depressed and worrying about something there is no need to worry. The truly knowledgeable ones will not worry about people who are alive or people who are dead. First of all Sri Krishna begins by scolding Arjuna - you are behaving like a learned man, a panditah. Pandits are of two types- one who is learned but no wisdom,

28

another one who has wisdom. The man without wisdom will base his actions not on experience but on theory, and his own understanding of a situation. A truly learned man, a man with real wisdom will not worry about things which are trivial. The Mahabharata war is a war in which a lot of people are going to die and only some will survive, so Sri Krishna is telling Arjuna, a truly wise person will not cry for those who are dead or those who are alive. Why not?

This war is fought on the basis of righteousness, it is a Dharma Yuddha. Arjuna has come here as a warrior to uphold what is righteous, what isDharma, he is here to perform his duty. When a doctor performs a surgery on a patient as a duty, there are chances of the. But the doctor should do his best, not worry. Similarly in this war there are many people who are going to die. Those who are on the side of *adharma*, unrighteousness, die, no need to cry, because they have participated in *adharma*. Their relatives may become depressed because they are experiencing their karmic impressions. They should not have gone to war on the side of *adharma*.

Here Sri Krishna as a teacher goes to the root of the problem rather than giving a superficial motivational talk. He starts getting into real issues. A doctor, when he examines a patient for a stomach ache, can treat the patient for symptoms. But a good doctor will get into the depth, understand the root cause of the problem and try to address it. Sri Krishna is doing the same with Arjuna. His root problem is lack of knowledge of the Self. What is the real Self? What is righteousness? Arjuna's fundamental problem is his identification with the body, mind and intellect. Arjuna feels that if he kills somebody he will be committing a sin. But he has forgotten that the real purpose of coming to war is to uphold Dharma. A Judge has to perform his duties whether it is a criminal, friend, foe or enemy. Similarly Arjuna has to perform his duties but he is not able to do that because of attachment to the body.

Sri Krishna seeks to remove the ignorance we have regarding the body - we think that anything happening to the body is happening to us, in reality it is not so. The real me is consciousness which has no birth, death or injury. Whenever we do namaskara, or offer something to someone, or communicate with others, it's not with the body that we do so, it is with the consciousness within. The consciousness is freed of birth and death, it cannot be destroyed.

But Arjuna is confused about his real identity, and the identity of the warriors in front of him. During festival season, an elephant carries the idol of deity and parades all over town. Devotees offer flowers and do namaskara to the deity, but the elephant thinks all that respect is offered to it. It forgets all about the deity on its back. Similarly our ego, which is identified with the body and mind, feels that everything is happening to 'me'. All communication is for 'me'; in reality communication is not for ego but it is for the Self within. Sri Krishna is giving this wisdom to Arjuna. Arjuna knows Sri Krishna as a relative, a friend and as a divine being. Until now Sri Krishna had not given any spiritual knowledge to Arjuna. Only when Arjuna surrenders to Sri Krishna and says, I am your disciple, please advise me, Sri Krishna gives him spiritual knowledge.

This is a true teacher. As a relative one can give only advice, as a friend one can give consolation, it cannot be wisdom. But when Arjuna accepts Sri Krishna as a Guru, as a spiritual teacher, only then does Sri Krishna advise him. Spiritual teaching can only come from a Guru, *'Gurumukhena vidya'*. Many of us go to some discourses, learn something from it, find it very appealing, and we try to teach it to others. But that may not go down well with them because they are not in the receptive mode. To be receptive one has to accept you as a Guru or a teacher, only then can knowledge transmission or wisdom transmission happen. For any spiritual education the student has to approach the master and seek to become a disciple, and only if the master accepts him/her as a disciple, wisdom transmission can happen. Otherwise it is a relationship like any other relationship - friend or relative. So Sri Krishna takes the position of a Guru for teaching Arjuna.

sri bhagavān uvācha,
aśhochyān-anvaśhochas-tvam
prajñā-vādānśh cha bhāṣhase I
Gatāsūn-agatāsūnśh-cha
nānuśhochanti paṇḍitāḥ II2.11II

****

Shloka 2.12

Never was there a time when I did not exist, nor you, nor all these kings; nor in the future shall any of us cease to be

Sri Krishna says, O' Arjuna both myself and yourself, and these kings - we were all there in the past, all of us will continue to be there in the future. Sri Krishna brings in one important concept of Indian philosophy here - the concept of rebirth. We consider life itself as a continuous process. The soul is immortal, it takes different bodies, experiences life and drops the body. Dropping the body is called death. The soul then takes a new body and starts living again, collecting more experiences, and this process will continue. Sri Krishna existed in the past, Arjuna existed in the past, all those kings existed in the past, you existed in the past… and all of them will continue to exist in the future too.

If you consider the soul as the body then this explanation will not apply. The soul is different from the body, the soul uses the body as a vehicle. Just like you change your car, the soul changes the body. Where were you before birth? You existed as consciousness or ātma before birth. The body you have taken now is called birth. When you drop this body it is called death. But birth and death are not for the soul. The soul will migrate to another body to experience life. This is the message of Sri Krishna.

There are many belief systems in the world that have a view that life is only this lifetime, there is no past or no future. There is no concept of rebirth in their belief system. This doesn't appear to be a scientific understanding. However there are many studies done by psychologists by what they call hypnosis. By hypnotizing someone they can go to their past birth to find where the person was born. Thorough studies have been done of which details are available, a person's past birth is traced. So the belief that this is the only birth seems to be not founded on a scientific basis. What is the implication of rebirth? If you understand that life is a continuity, we take birth to fulfill a certain purpose. So we will be more responsible towards life and our actions, because whatever we do in this lifetime, we will get back in future lifetimes. But if we consider birth as an event restricted to this life alone, then there will be a lot of pressure on us to extract the maximum juice out of life, it puts stress and it is out of tune with the scientific reality.

na tvevāhaṁ jātu nāsaṁ
na tvaṁ neme janādhipāḥ I
na chaiva na bhaviṣhyāmaḥ
sarve vayamataḥ param II2.12II

****

Shloka 2.13

The body naturally passes from childhood to youth and old age. Similarly, at the time of death, the soul passes from one body to another. The wise are not deluded by this transition.

There is no birth or death for the Ātman which uses the body as a vehicle to experience life. We know that a vehicle like a car has a manufacturing date. After 10 – 12 years we say that the car is old. When it becomes too old to use it is junked. However, the driver of that car is not junked! He buys another car and starts driving it. Similarly, the Ātman is the driver who uses the body-mind- intellect complex as a vehicle. At the time of death, the Ātman moves from one vehicle to another.

The body is subject to birth, growth, decay and death. It goes through phases like youth, old age and disease. Do not confuse the changing body with the changeless ātman. The Self has no birth or death. You are that changeless ātman, Self. Though characteristics of the body are superimposed on the Self, do not confuse yourself with the changing body which is only a vehicle.

In the shloka, Krishna uses the word *dhīrāh* or 'courageous one' to describe an enlightened being or Jñānī. A Jñānī is courageous because he is not afraid or deluded by death. He knows that he is the immortal Self. He never confuses the Self with the non-Self. The body is the non-Self. The body is the vehicle and the Self is the driver.

dehino-asmin yathā dehe
kaumāram yauvanam jarā I
tathā dehāntara-prāptir
dhīrāh tatra na muhyati II2.13II

****

Shloka 2.14

O Son of Kunti, the contact between senses and sense objects gives rise to perceptions like heat and cold, pleasure and pain. These are transient in nature. They rise and fall. Therefore learn to be patient and withstand this duality. Don't be affected by it.

The very nature of life is duality. Everything occurs in pairs. We have darkness and light, pleasure and pain, happiness and unhappiness. But we love pleasant things and hate unpleasant ones. We crave happiness and run away from pain. However, life doesn't guarantee that we always get what we want. Neither does it burden us continuously with what we don't want. It keeps oscillating between the two because life is energy and the nature of Shakti or energy is 'change'.

Yes, Shakti or energy is constantly moving, constantly changing. The situations in our lives also change from moment to moment. We experience pleasure or pain when our senses come in contact with stimuli. By itself, this fluctuation is not wrong. Life is like that. But the problem is that such contacts leave deep rooted impressions called samskāras in our consciousness. When something traumatic happens, it imprints itself on our consciousness. Our memory functions like a hard disk where everything that occurs is recorded as an impression. Though the experience of pleasure or pain is momentary, the imprint or samskāra it leaves behind is long lasting. It exerts pressure on us and forces us to do certain things in life. It makes us seek pleasure and shun pain. So we become slaves of external circumstances. It is as though we have handed the world a remote device to control us.

When we allow pleasure to create elation and pain to create depression in us, there is constant turbulence inside. The greater the turbulence, the more the impressions. Instead of oscillating constantly, it would make a great difference if we witness pleasure and pain with equanimity with the awareness that they are both temporary. When we develop equanimity, no imprints are generated in our consciousness.

Of course, we have to live in the world. That is not really the problem. It is when the world starts living in us that the problem begins. The moment our experiences in the world create samskāras, the world is living in us. The imprint in us is the source of the problem. Craving and resistance leave impressions in our consciousness and these Samskāras turn us into puppets of circumstances. So learn to live without creating impressions. That is why scriptures praise the lotus. This beautiful flower which is born in slime, grows in water and blooms in sunlight. Despite this, the lotus does not have a single characteristic of the slime in which it is born. That is why it is a symbol of enlightened living. That is how we should live.

We too are born in a society where there is both good and bad. We should not be affected by this because this is the nature of society. We should bloom into beautiful individuals. The water where the lotus blooms can be compared to the many things that happen in the world around us. We should not be attached to them. The Sun represents wisdom - the wisdom to be in this world but not of this world. This is the path to liberation.

That is why Sri Krishna tells Arjuna, "O Arjuna, don't be affected by the dualities of life. Learn to be a witness. Live life with equanimity and be free."

mātrā-sparśhāh tu kaunteya
śhītoṣhṇa-sukha-duḥkha-dāḥ
āgamāpāyino-anityāh
tāms-titikṣhasva bhārata II2.14II

****

Shlokas 2.20, 2.22, 2.23

The soul is neither born, nor does it ever die; nor having once existed, does it ever cease to be. The soul is without birth, eternal, immortal, and ageless. It is not destroyed when the body is destroyed [2.20]

Just as a person sheds worn-out garments and wears new ones, at the time of death the soul casts off its worn-out body and enters a new one [2.22]

Weapons cannot shred the soul, nor can fire burn it. Water cannot wet it, nor can wind dry it [2.23]

There is a great difference between the body and the Self. We understood that the body is a vehicle of the Self and the Self is the driver of the body. Now let's look at another example. A light bulb cannot emit light without the power of electricity. In the same way, the body remains inert if it is not powered by the Self. The Self is consciousness and the body is inert. You also understood that you are not the body. You are the Self. You are Consciousness.

So do not confuse yourself with the body. The body has a birthday. It will also die one day. But the Self, which is consciousness, was never born. Neither will it die. Though it associates with the mortal body, it is immortal. Fire cannot burn consciousness. Water cannot wet it and wind cannot dry it because it is non-material in nature. It is completely unaffected by anything that happens in the world.

Let's look at another example. You buy a beautiful dress from a store and wear it. As time passes, the dress becomes old and faded. Then you get tired of it and throw it away. In the same way, the Self uses the body as a vehicle for many years. When it becomes old and useless, the Self casts it away and takes on another body. Things that happen in the world affect the body, but never the Self within. Don't confuse yourself with the mortal body. You are the Self. You are eternally free.

na jāyate mriyate vā kadāchin
nāyaṁ bhūtvā bhavitā vā na bhūyaḥ I
ajo nityaḥ shāshvatoyaṁ purāṇo
na hanyate hanyamāne sharīre II2.20II

vāsānsi jīrṇāni yathā vihāya
navāni gṛihṇāti naro 'parāṇi I
tathā sharīrāṇi vihāya jīrṇāya
nyāni sanyāti navāni dehī II2.21II

nainaṁ chhindanti śhastrāṇi
nainaṁ dahati pāvakaḥ I
na chainaṁ kledayantyāpo
na śhoṣhayati mārutaḥ II2.23II

****

Shlokas 2.27, 2.30

Death is guaranteed for one who is born, and rebirth is inevitable for one who has died. Therefore, you should not lament over the inevitable (2.27)

O Arjuna, the soul that dwells within the body is immortal; therefore, you should not mourn for anyone (2.30)

Everyone who is born is sure to die. No one can escape death. As we have already seen, death means merely changing the old body for a new one. This is called rebirth. This cycle of birth-death-rebirth is called *punarapi jananam punarapi maranam punarapi janani jatare shayanam*. It keeps repeating itself endlessly. Though it seems like an insoluble problem, there is a solution. When we realize I am not the perishable body but the eternal Self, we exit this cycle.

We are born because we have desires to fulfill. In order to do this, we use the vehicle called the body. In the process of fulfilling our existing desires, we generate many new ones. So it becomes impossible to fulfill our innumerable desires in one lifetime. Therefore we take up another body. This process of having desires and fulfilling them is called the cycle of Karma. It is almost impossible to exit this cycle. Those who understand their true nature and exit this cycle are the liberated ones, *muktas*. These are extremely rare. The bulk of humanity is trapped in this cycle and takes thousands of lifetimes to evolve and be liberated. That is why Sri Krishna asks Arjuna, "O Arjuna, why are you worried?"

As we have now understood, though the Self resides in a perishable body, it is immortal. It migrates from one body to another. That is why we should not worry about death. Sri Ramakrishna Paramahamsa illustrates this with a parable. A fisherman throws a net into the sea to catch fish. Some fish are too wise to enter the net. Some are caught, but jump out of the net. The fish that are caught cannot escape. This is also what happens to most living beings. They are trapped in the net called illusion or māya because they confuse themselves thinking that they are the perishable body. So they move from one body to another seeking to fulfill their endless desires. Those who understand that they are the eternal Self and not the body jump out from the net of māya. They are called *Jivanmuktas*. They are too wise to get trapped in māya. That is why Sri Krishna asks Arjuna, "Why are you crying over this insoluble problem?"

jātasya hi dhruvo mṛityur
dhruvaṁ janma mṛitasya cha I
tasmād aparihārye 'rthe
na tvaṁ śhochitum arhasi II2.27II

dehī nityam avadhyo 'yaṁ
dehe sarvasya bhārata I
tasmāt sarvāṇi bhūtāni
na tvaṁ śhochitum arhasi II2.30II

****

Shloka 2.40

Working in this state of consciousness, there is no loss or adverse result, and even a little effort saves one from great danger

To give him confidence, Sri Krishna tells Arjuna, "If you do even a little bit of selfless service or *nishkāmaKarma*, you will be free from great fear. The wonderful thing is that even if you are unable to complete the task or accomplish it perfectly, there are no adverse effects.

What does this mean? What is the great fear Sri Krishna talks about? Let's see. When we begin any challenging task, we may think, "What if I am not able to complete it? Will there be some adverse effect if I can't do this perfectly?" This happens because we depend solely on our ability. It may also happen when we do something for our own benefit. This insecurity and anxiety about the result of our actions is resolved if we do everything as a selfless act of service or *nishkāmaKarma*. When we perform each task with the feeling that it is an offering to God and accept the result as his prasādam or grace, we are free from the fear of whether we will succeed in our ventures or not. Even death does not scare us anymore.

For example, let us say, I start constructing a house. If I am unable to complete it, then all the effort I have put is gone. The money that I have invested is wasted. This is my main fear when I start the house. But in the case of *nishkāmaKarma*, there is no such fear. Whatever I receive as the outcome of every task is God's *prasādam.*

That is true for all spiritual activity. Whatever spiritual activity we do, we may not be able to do it 100% perfectly. But even the little we do relieves us from the fear of the outcome. Conversely, those who don't engage in *nishkāmaKarma* have a lot of stress and tension in life.

nehābhikrama-nāśho'sti
pratyavāyo na vidyate I
svalpamapi asyaDharmasya
trāyate mahato bhayāt II2.40II

****

Shloka 2.41

Those who are on this path are resolute in purpose, and their aim is one. O' beloved child of the Kurus, the intelligence of those who are irresolute is many-branched

O' Arjuna! For those who are focused on Karma Yoga their mind is one-pointed. Whereas those who are not doing Karma Yoga they are actually a confused lot. And they will try many things.

In life, anybody with a clear focus and clarity will act purposefully, whereas those who don't have clarity will try many things. And each of them will give limited results. But the person who is focused on Karma Yoga has such clarity that he takes firm steps and moves in the path of Karma Yoga.

Let us look at an example – For what reason does anybody work in life -*Dharma, artha, kāma, moksha.*
dharma means for righteousness, *artha* means money, *kāma* means desire and *moksha* means liberation. For these purposes anybody works in life. These are the basic motivations. A person who works only for money, such a person's mind is not firm. Say, if somebody offers him a little more money, then his mind gets diverted from his present work. That's because his focus is only money. He is doing something else and somebody offers him more money he will get diverted. And if someone offers him less, then he gets agitated as well. Such a mind is not focused.

Whereas for a person who is involved in Karma Yoga nothing can stop him because his focus is not the result or immediate result or his focus is not the money. He is working on all his activities as an offering to God, as a service to God. And anything that comes as a result, good or bad, he accepts it as prasādam or a gift from God. Because of the fact that he is focused while working, he is not disturbed when he gets the result also. That cannot be seen in someone who is not focused - because of the diversion the results are also poor.

It is like this - somebody wants to dig a well, and he starts digging; he digs for 20 feet and finds no water.

So, he digs another well and he keeps on digging multiple wells. Whereas a person who knows where the water is will dig deep and within a 100 feet he will get water. Whereas the other person has dug 20 wells but nowhere he could find water. A Karma Yogi is like that. He knows exactly why he is doing and what he is doing and he is very focused. His purpose is not the immediate result but the 'Divine Grace'.

vyavasāyātmikā buddhir
ekeha kuru-nandana I
bahu-śhākhā hyanantāśh cha
buddhayo 'vyavasāyinām II2.41II

****

Shloka 2.44

In the minds of those who are too attached to sense enjoyment and material opulence, and who are bewildered by such things, the resolute determination of devotional service to the Supreme Lord does not take place

Those who engage in activities for the sake of bhoga, which means enjoyment and aishwarya, which means wealth, cannot become calm or attain samadhi. They find it difficult to reach the state of inner bliss where one can realize God. For such people, it is very difficult to realize God.

Whatever type of work we do affects us. Because we get involved in the work intensely and that intensity leaves impressions in our mind. It could be any work - a businessman, a doctor or an engineer. There are many different professions, but people work for only two reasons: Bhoga for enjoyment; I want to get this, I want to get that. We are motivated by bhoga. Aishwarya- for more and more richness. We are motivated by aishwarya.

Whenever we do something, some results can be favorable or some can be unfavorable. If the result is favorable, we get elated which in turn leaves impressions in our mind, and we get motivated to do more work. If the result is unfavorable, we get depressed. Either way it starts affecting us if we are bhoga or aishwarya oriented. But it's not true for a person who is service oriented or who is involved in Karma Yoga. He performs all actions as an offering to God, as a service to God and any fruits come for the Karma favorable or unfavorable, he accepts it as a gift from Divine. Because of this his mind becomes more and more calm and peaceful. When it becomes calm and peaceful then the mind gets purified. And because his mind gets purified his intellect is not wavering anymore. And because of that he attains the calmness which is required for meditation and attains that supreme bliss which is his own nature. For supreme realization he can focus his mind.

I had a friend who was working for almost 12 years in the software industry. Sometime ago he left his job and I asked him why. He said that he was in the testing industry and testing means finding fault with a software. Working so hard in the industry gradually his mind became only a fault-finding sort of mind. When he was at his home, he only found fault while he was talking to his wife, when he was talking to his children, he was finding fault. The attitude of his profession seeped deep inside and that it had started affecting his personal life also. So, he felt enough is enough and quit his job. He said, "It was actually affecting my personal life. My mind was becoming more of a fault-finding one instead of a constructive mind. So, I decided to quit and do something else".

Similarly, whatever work we do affects the way we think, affects our consciousness, affects our mind. The best way to do any work is Karma Yoga. Do any work, either small or big as an offering to God, as a service to God, as a purpose for purification of yourself. Work will be beautiful and gradually the mind will become calm and will lead to supreme realization of God within you.

bhogaiśwvarya-prasaktānāṁ
tayāpahṛita-chetasām I
vyavasāyātmikā buddhiḥ
samādhau na vidhīyate II2.44II

****

Shloka 2.45

The Vedas deal with three modes of material nature, O Arjuna. Rise above the three modes to a state of pure spiritual consciousness. Freeing yourself from dualities, eternally fixed in Truth, and without concern for material gain and safety, be situated in the Self

Material Nature consists of three modes or gunas – *sattva, rajas and tamas.* Sattva is a mode or an attitude where purity and selflessness prevail. When we are sattvic we always consider the interests of other people and try to engage ourselves in activities that benefit the world. We are calm and joyful. If we operate in the mode of rajas, we are result oriented. We do something to help others only if it also benefits us. In the tamasic mode, we are self centered. We want to fulfill our own needs at the expense of others. We are also resistant to change. The spiritual path is designed to take us on the upward spiral from tamas and rajas to sattva. Ultimately the sattva mode also has to be transcended as it still induces a sense of doer-ship in us.

The Vedas also create a framework for these three modes. The *Rig, Yajur, Atharva and Sāma Vedas* have a portion called Karma Kanda. This describes different kinds of rituals and their outcomes. There are rituals prescribed for acquiring wealth, for begetting children, attaining heaven after death and so on. All of them are done for getting merit either here while we are alive or hereafter, when we die.

When we do a puja or ritual at home, we begin with an affirmation or sankalpa. We may place a big list before God when we do this – I want a good job, more money, a car, a house and so on. Such rituals are called *kāmya Karma.* We are performing the ritual for some personal benefit. So, here our modes of action are tamas and rajas. We are still operating under the forces of like and dislike. We perform the rituals because we want to acquire something or because we want to avoid something. This is fine for those who wish to satisfy worldly ambitions.

However, if we are focussing on Self Knowledge, it is better to perform rituals with the intention of purifying ourselves, and as a sincere offering to God rather than to fulfill a materialistic desire. This brings about self-purification and establishes us in sattva guna.

Witnessing also takes us to sattva mode. Instead of getting involved in our likes and dislikes, it is better to witness them calmly. The more we witness, the more peaceful and joyful we become. When we are sattvic, we are able to focus on the quest for Self Knowledge and realize our true nature.

trai-guṇya-viṣhayā vedā
nistrai-guṇyo bhavārjuna I
nirdvandvo nitya-sattva-stho
niryoga-kṣhema ātmavān II2.45II

****

Shloka 2.47

You have a right to perform your prescribed duties, but you are not entitled to the fruits of your actions. Never consider yourself to be the cause of the results of your activities, nor be attached to inaction

Sri Krishna says, "O Arjuna! You have a right to do your duty but you have no control over the fruits of your actions. So don't get attached to them. Don't run away from your responsibilities either. You should love doing your duty, but drop your attachment to its results."

Let's look at an example. Everyone wants to score 100 percent in the exams. Suppose a boy who has to prepare for his exams says, "I will study only if I get a guarantee that I will score 100 percent." Who can give him such a guarantee? If he constantly focuses on the results, he is unable to study properly. Scoring 100 percent is the end result of his studying and writing the exam. He may fall sick or the question paper may be tough. The examiner may not evaluate his paper properly. He has no control over many such factors that govern his results. So if he focuses on all this, he begins to worry constantly, "Will I get 100 percent or not? Will the question paper be easy? Will my paper be evaluated fairly?" Then his concentration is disturbed and he can't absorb what he is studying.

So what should he do? While studying and writing his exam he should focus on those activities exclusively, setting aside all speculation about the results. Then he is sure to prepare and perform well in the exams. The results may or may not fulfill his expectations. If he scores less than he expected, he should not get depressed but accept it calmly and enthusiastically explore the options that are open to him. This becomes easy to do only when he is not attached to the results.

In a way this shloka summarizes the entire teaching of the Bhagavad Gita. What is the summary? We should carry out all our responsibilities to the best of our ability and accept the outcome as the grace of God. Sri Krishna says, "Karma manifests both through the individual and the universe. You do your part and the universe will do its part. The final outcome of any action depends on your karmic impressions and their impact. Since you cannot always predict this beforehand, simply accept the results as God's grace." Look at how a surgeon works. In a critical case, he doesn't know whether the surgery will save his patient or not. But that doesn't stop him from performing the operation to the best of his ability.

Sri Krishna's message is extremely practical. Focus on your ability, work for the best result but don't get attached to it. This is the way to purify ourselves. This is the way to perform Karma yoga and offer each action to God.

Karmaṇy-evādhikāras te
mā phaleṣhu kadāchana I
mā Karma-phala-hetur bhūr
mā te saṅgo 'stvaKarmaṇi II2.47II

****

Shloka 2.59

Aspirants may restrain the senses from their objects of enjoyment, but the taste for the sense objects remains. However, even this taste ceases for those who realize the Supreme

In the earlier shlokas of this chapter we have discussed different aspects of Karma Yoga. Karma Yoga includes the paths of Kriya, Bhakti and Jnāna Yoga. Wherever action is directed towards Self Realization, it qualifies as Karma Yoga. An aspirant on the path is called a Yogi. Since he does everything without attachment to the fruits of action, he gets purified. He also stops indulging in sense objects. However his inner hankering does not vanish till he realizes his true nature. This is easy to understand if we take the example of a diabetic. He is very fond of sweets, but his doctor tells him to stop eating them. Physically he reduces his intake of sugar, but his desire to eat sweets is still present inside. It is like a ticking bomb can surface anytime and lead him into trouble.

This is not the case with a Jnani who is equipoised. His heart is full of bliss all the time. His happiness no longer depends on sense objects outside. While we associate happiness with outer experiences, he knows that his true nature is bliss. So whether he comes in contact with sense objects or not, his internal craving to get joy from them has completely disappeared.

The enlightened Master, Sri Ramakrishna loved eating sweets. His wife Sharada Devi scolded him saying, "Self Realization means dropping all cravings, but you go on eating sweets. So many people come here to get your blessings and wisdom. What will they think when they see you indulging yourself in this way?" Sri Ramakrishna said, "What you say is true for a seeker on the path. He identifies so strongly with the body that it is difficult for him to completely drop his cravings. He finds it very tough to establish himself firmly in the Self. However, here the case is very different. I identify with the Self all the time. My bond to the body is very tenuous and can break anytime. My work here is not yet done. Many of my disciples are yet to come to me. In order to retain this body till my mission is complete, I have to hold on to some cravings."

So, a Jnāni has drunk the nectar of Self Knowledge. For him everything else is insipid. Only the Self exists and nothing else. Everything is an expression of the Self alone. So where is the question of having craving or repulsion?

viṣhayā vinivartante
nirāhārasya dehinaḥ I
Rasa-varjaṁ raso'pyasya
paraṁ dṛiṣhṭvā nivartate II2.59II

****

Shlokas 2.62, 2.63

While contemplating the objects of the senses, a person develops attachment for them, and from such attachment lust develops, and from lust anger arises. (2.62)

From anger, delusion arises, and from delusion bewilderment of memory. When memory is bewildered, intelligence is lost, and when intelligence is lost, one falls down again into the material pool. (2.63)

In these two Shlokas, Sri Krishna tells Arjuna WHAT how anger affects us. Anger disturbs us and when we get angry, we lose our awareness. When in anger, people do unspeakable activities and later they start regretting. So the process of getting angry is described here.

dhyāyataḥ viṣhayān puṁsaḥ - constantly thinking of objects, sense objects. *saṅgas teṣhūpajāyate* - He gets attached to that. *saṅgāt sañjāyate kāmaḥ* - because of the attachment, there is desire, *kāmāt krodho 'bhijāyate* - when there is a desire and if you can get that object, your desire will be fulfilled. But if you cannot get that object, then there is frustration which causes anger. What is the problem when anger rises?

krodhād bhavati sammohaḥ - with anger comes forgetfulness of one's nature. *sammohāt smṛiti-vibhramaḥ* - When he forgets his own nature, the intellect is destroyed, logical thinking and processing is gone - he's not able to think logically and that person falls down, his downfall begins.

I read about a famous case in Indian crime history. There was a great officer who won many medals in the military. After retirement, one day, when he returned home from outside, he saw his wife with someone else. He gets angry, takes his revolver and shoots both of them. After a few moments, when his anger came down, he realized what he had done and started regretting. He was arrested and he spent the rest of life in prison.

So when people get angry, they don't know what they are doing. They do unspeakable things. Anger is something which we have to overcome. The problem with anger is, if you suppress it, it will hurt you, if you express it, it will hurt somebody else. So you should learn the art of transcending the anger - Going beyond the anger. Sri Krishna tells the process of how anger rises. If you get exposed to some sense objects constantly, you develop attachment and from that attachment, desire for the object increases.

This is typically used by the marketing agencies where they constantly expose you to the advertisements. Whether it is a car or TV or a fridge or any food items. By constant exposure, you start getting attracted to that and you desire to purchase that object. When you get that object, you will feel happy. But if you are not able to get that object, you get frustrated and anger arises.

What is the problem if you get angry? When the anger arises, there is a forgetfulness of your own nature. Whether you are an officer, or employee or husband or wife, you forget your own nature. When you forget your own nature, your intellect doesn't work logically. Intellect gets destroyed, in that sense. You don't know what you are doing, and you commit crimes, or hurt others. You might throw objects or even break them. One person brought a beautiful imported watch, and in a fit of anger he threw it, and that watch broke into pieces.

We have to understand the root cause of anger and overcome anger. Suppression is not the solution, expression is not the solution, we have to transcend anger. This is the message of Sri Krishna.

dhyāyato viṣhayān puṁsaḥ
saṅgas teṣhūpajāyate I
saṅgāt sañjāyate kāmaḥ
kāmāt krodho 'bhijāyate II2.62II

krodhād bhavati sammohaḥ
sammohāt smṛiti-vibhramaḥ I
smṛiti-bhranśhād buddhi-nāśho
buddhi-nāśhāt praṇaśhyati II2.63II

****

Shloka 2.64

But one who controls the mind, and is free from attachment and aversion, even while using the objects of the senses, attains the Grace of God

rāga-dveṣha-viyuktaih - raga and dvesha means attraction and repulsion, so, one who has become free from attraction and repulsion. *vidheyātmā* - Atma means antahkarana, inner consciousness, the mind. He keeps the mind under his control. *Indriyaih viṣhayān* - while his mind is under control, he can still experience the objects through the sense organs. But, *prasādam adhigachchhati* - the mind itself will always be calm and peaceful. So this is the state of a realized person.

A Yogi stays away from sense objects, why? Because it can create attraction and repulsion, which can lead to anger and other undesirable effects, which can disturb the mind. Now the Yogi has reached the stage where he has realized his Self. When he has realized his Self, the mind is under the control of the Self, the mind has become calm. Now he can enjoy the sense objects again, because there is no fear of slipping. Something like a doctor prescribing medicines to a patient, "you have a stomach upset, don't eat such-and-such foods because they can cause disturbance in the stomach". So the patient follows it faithfully, and after a while he has recovered from the stomach ache. Now the doctor says, 'you can eat now, because there is no impact". Similarly during the process of Sadhana, one can abstain from sense objects. By that process he makes his mind calm and after making his mind calm, he realizes his Self, after Self Realization nothing else matters to him. He can as well be free from sense objects. But since he is in a state of *rāga-dveṣha-viyuktaih* - he is free from attraction and repulsion - the sense object itself doesn't cause any harm to him. So now he can enjoy sense objects, but mind is not agitated or disturbed.

This is the state of a realized person. In the state of realization, there's neither attraction or repulsion, whereas in the state of Sadhana, "Oh, I don't want to take that" - there is a repulsion because that can cause a repulsion in the mind. For a Jnani, to all sense objects there is no attraction or repulsion. For example, many Yogis meditate in order to attain Sri Krishna, to realize God. They follow celibacy, Brahmacharya, because they want to make their mind calm and realize the God within. But Sri Krishna himself is a married person, right? But for Him, there is neither attraction or repulsion. One who is troubled by attraction and repulsion has to abstain from sense objects so as to make his mind calm. A realized person goes beyond the attraction and repulsion. This is the message of this shloka.

rāga-dveṣha-viyuktais tu
viṣhayān indriyaiśh charan I
ātma-vaśhyair-vidheyātmā
prasādam adhigachchhati II2.64II

****

Shloka 2.69

What all beings consider as day is the night of ignorance for the wise, and what all creatures see as night is the day for the introspective sage

yā niśhā sarva-bhūtānāṁ - that which is night for or all living beings - *tasyāṁ jāgarti sanyamī* - an Enlightened one, or Stithapragna will be alert in that, awake in that. *yasyāṁ jāgrati bhūtāni* - all living beings, in whatever they think as daylight are awake - *sā niśhā paśhyato muneḥ* - that an Enlightened one sees as the darkness or night. A paradoxical statement, it's a paradoxical verse.

What is seen as daylight, or condition of awareness or awakening for the living beings, is seen as the darkness or night by the enlightened one. On the other hand, what is seen as night by living beings, is seen as light or day by the enlightened one. How is it possible? The two are contradictory, right? This is the state of an enlightened being. What is real for all living beings is unreal for an enlightened one, what is unreal for the enlightened one is real for the other living beings. So what is this?

There are two aspects of our being. One is the outer world - the world of sense objects, and the other is the state of the inner world, the state of Atma. So most living beings, in their ignorance, forget their Self nature and identify with the sense objects. The sense objects are real for them. The Self or Atma is unreal for them. What is real is called 'light' and what is unreal is called 'darkness'. On the other hand, for the enlightened being, the Self is very much real and the non-self, meaning sense objects, are nothing but an appearance in the Self. So for him Atma or the Self is the 'light', or the state of awareness, whereas the sense objects are 'darkness'. So that is why there is a contrast in the experience of an ordinary human being, living being, and an enlightened one.

The enlightened one sees the world as sense objects or māya or appearance. Like a mirage in the desert. The mirage appears to be like water, and people rush towards it. They try to drink water from that to quench their thirst, where there is no water! But water appears to be real and they rush towards the mirage. Whereas a person who knows it is a mirage doesn't get attracted - he knows it is a mirage and doesn't rush towards that. An enlightened being is one who doesn't rush towards sense objects, doesn't get attracted to sense objects because he knows it is an appearance, it is not real. On the other hand, unrealized people are attracted to sense objects.

This is a state of a realized being versus the state of an unrealized being. There is a story about a master called Gurdjieff. He had a student called Ouspensky. Gurdjieff was a Russian master, Ouspensky was the chief disciple. Ouspensky comes to Gurdjieff and says. "Master, I want to learn meditation". So Gurdjieff puts a condition, "If you want to learn meditation, you have to practice it in isolation for three months, in these three months you should not meet anybody, you should be away from the society". Ouspensky says yes and he stays away and practices meditation. After three months, he comes back to the master, master Gurdjieff. Gurdjieff says, "let us go for a walk". So when they go for a walk, Ouspensky says, "Master, why are people sleep-walking in the city?". To him, now everybody seems to be sleep-walking! Gurdjieff says, "Great, now you have awakened. Because you have awakened you see these people sleep-walking. Three months ago, you were also walking like them, and you thought everything was normal".

When I say sleep-walking, I mean people are walking without awareness of their Self. Whereas Ouspensky, after the meditation practice, had become aware of his real Self. That is why all enlightened beings are called 'Awakened' beings. They've woken up from the dream - the dream called māya or the appearance.

yā niśhā sarva-bhūtānāṁ
tasyāṁ jāgarti sanyamī I
yasyāṁ jāgrati bhūtāni
sā niśhā paśhyato muneḥ II2.69II

****

CHAPTER 3: KARMA YOGA

Shloka 3.3

The Lord said: O sinless one, the two paths leading to enlightenment were previously explained by me: the path of knowledge, for those inclined towards contemplation, and the path of work for those inclined towards action

O' Arjuna, *loke asmin* - in this world there are two paths- *dvividha nishta*, as I have told you earlier - *pura prokta maya nagha - jnānayogena Sānkhyanam* - there is the path of *Sānkhyas, Jnāna yoga, and Karma yogena Yoginam* - the path of Karma yoga followed by Karma Yogis.

Sri Krishna is telling Arjuna about the two paths of self realization, Jnāna yoga followed by Sānkhyas, and Karma yoga followed by Yogis. So now the question comes, "Oh! We have heard of multiple paths. We have heard *Karma Yoga, Bhakti Yoga, Kriya Yoga, Raja Yoga and Jnāna Yoga* - what about all those other paths? Why is Sri Krishna mentioning only two paths?"

Karma Yoga means Path of Action. Everything you do, whenever you act and do something, it falls in the category of Karma Yoga. There are four different

types of actions you can perform. These actions are
kāyā, vāchā, manasā and buddhyā.

kāyā means you can do some action using your
physical body. vāchā means you can do something
verbally. manasā means you can do something
mentally. buddhyā means you can do something with
your buddhi or intellect. So, all these four fall into the
category of Karma Yoga because there are four
actions - physical, verbal, mental, intellectual.

Physical action means devotional service and *yajna*.
Then there is verbal action such as chanting or *japa*
or mantra chanting. There are different types of
chanting and prayers and they come under the
category of verbal action called vāchā. Then mental
action is nothing but meditation and buddhyā -
intellectual action is the study of scriptures and
understanding of scriptures. Physical, mental, verbal,
intellectual activities all are classified into one
category called Karma Yoga because it involves
some action. This is the Path of Action.

So studying scriptures is also considered as Karma
Yoga. Others do prayers, meditation, kriya yoga,
which actually involves movement of energy through
āsana and prānayama, they all come under the
category of Karma Yoga and those who follow the
path of Karma Yoga are called Yogis.

There is another path, which is Path of Awareness. This is followed by people called Sānkhyas. What is the Path of Awareness? You become aware of what you are not. Understand that you are not 'that', and start going inwards until you reach your own Self. This is the path of neti, neti or not this, not this. In this path you realize what you are by dropping out what you are not; you will realize,

nānu nānembudu nānalla
ee deha mana buddhi nānalla
sachchidānandātma shiva nānu nāne
shivoham shivoham shivoham

I am not the what I think I am, I am not the body, mind, or intellect, I am Pure Consciousness, I am Shiva

You realize that you are not the body, not the mind, not the intellect, you are Consciousness, Chaitanya, Shiva-swaroopi, which is pure and auspicious. So, this you do by the process of elimination, by awareness, it is called Sānkhya yoga.

There are only two paths - Path of Awareness and Path of Action. Awareness is not action. So, what is the difference between Awareness and action? In action, if I do something, I cannot do something else.

For example, when I eat food, I cannot play cricket. When I watch a movie, I cannot write. When I study the scriptures, I cannot watch a movie. Thus action involves exclusive dedication from the body-mind and intellect to execute it.

But in the Path of Awareness, I can mix awareness with anything. When I walk, talk, drink…I can have awareness. Basically, Awareness goes with anything. Awareness of 'what I am not' and 'what I am' goes with anything. The Path of Awareness is Sānkhya Yoga.

There is an interesting story in Purānas: Lord Shiva and Goddess Parvathi were once resting in Kailasa. Their children Ganesha and Subramanya were playing with each other when Sage Narada visited and gave a mango fruit to Mother Parvathi. He said, "This fruit is very precious. You should not cut this fruit. You can only give this fruit to one person whom you think is wise", and left.

When both Ganesha and Subrahmanya tried to claim the fruit from themselves from their mother, she agreed, but on one condition, "whoever completes going around the earth three times and comes back first, will get this fruit" she said. Even before she could finish the sentence Subrahmanya hopped on to his vehicle, the peacock and set off around the earth.

Ganesha's vehicle was very small and slow, so he simply went around his divine parents Shiva and Parvathi, bowed down to them and said, "give me the fruit"! Impressed, Goddess Parvathi gave him the fruit.

When Subrahmanya comes back after completing three rounds of earth, he sees Ganesha eating the fruit and becomes furious. "How did he get the fruit?" he damns, "he did not even leave this place. He did not even try going around the earth even once. How can he get the mango?". Parvathi ask him to ask his brother about it, and Ganesha replies, "the entire universe is nothing but Consciousness; it boils down to Shiva - Consciousness, and Parvathi - Energy. The universe is the play of Shiva and Shakti, and I have gone round Shiva and Shakti, which means I have not just gone round the earth, but around the entire creation, entire universe thrice. That is why I deserve the fruit."

Here, Ganesha represents the Path of Wisdom, Sānkhya Yoga, and Subrahmanya represents Path of Yoga, Path of Action. For example, there is a massive tree which needs to be cut. Different people give different suggestions on how to cut the trees. Some say cut off the branches one by one, and cut the tree part by part, then finally cut the tree. One person gives a simple suggestion - just drill a hole into the root of the tree and cut off its roots, it will eventually kill the tree.

So, these are the two paths. The path of wisdom, the path of awareness is just going to the root of the problem, the root of our ignorance. "I am the body, I am the mind, I am the intellect" is the root of our problem and removing that through awareness is similar to cutting the root of the tree. But the difficulty is to locate the root, and cut it. So many people require the other path - where the tree has to be killed slowly.

The tree represents our Karmic impressions, ignorance and our life. So, all karmic impressions have to be cut one by one. For this, we need to go through the path of action - Karma Yoga, path of devotion - Bhakti Yoga, path of energy - Kriya Yoga and path of knowledge, Jnāna Yoga; they all lead to killing the tree slowly until it is finally uprooted. The tree is the Tree of samsāra.

sri bhagavān uvācha,
loke 'smin dvi-vidhā niṣhṭhā
purā proktā mayānagha I
jnāna-yogena sānkhyanāṁ
Karma-yogena Yoginām II3.3II

****

Shloka 3.9

Work has to be performed as an offering to Existence/Ishwara. Otherwise work causes bondage in this material world. Therefore, O' son of Kunti, perform your prescribed duties for His satisfaction, and in that way you will always remain free from bondage

Sri Krishna tells Arjuna the secret of Karma Yoga - perform actions as *yajna*. *yajna* implies the worship of fire, right? Putting things like ghee, rice, flowers etc into fire as an offering to God is a symbolic way of expressing devotion. Fire represents consciousness, and when all our actions are performed as offering to the divine, it becomes *yajna*, a service to the lord. Yajna is the basic principle of the universe. *yajna* is the way the universe works. Everything in the universe works as an offering.

For example, the ocean gives water to the clouds, clouds pour the water into rivers, rivers pour the water into the ocean… everything in the universe is working to offer something to existence. Similarly, when we start working with our actions as an offering to existence, as an offering to the divine, we will become free from the bondage of Karma. Karma itself will lead to karmic impressions, which in turn lead to more Karma and more bondage. This is the normal way of Karma. So Karma Yoga frees us from the bondage of Karma.

For example if you drive on the wrong side of the road, policemen will catch you. If you are going on the right side of the road, nobody will bother you. Similarly, the universe - existence - will give Karma phala or puts you into bondage if you do not follow the laws of the universe. However not all actions cause bondage. If you work according to the laws of the universe, you'll be free from bondage. The laws of the universe, or the operation of the universe is determined by the principle called *yajna*. *yajna* is a seva, *yajna* is an offering. Seeing the divine in all living beings, performing actions as a devotional service to God, not attached to the results of the action, is called *yajna*. Only those who live based on the principle of *yajna* will become free from the karmic bondage. This is the secret of Karma Yoga.

yajñārthāt Karmaṇo 'nyatra
loko 'yaṁ Karma-bandhanaḥ ll
tad-arthaṁ Karma kaunteya
mukta-saṅgaḥ samācara ll3.9ll

****

Shloka 3.14

All living beings subsist on food, and food is produced by rains. Rains come from the performance of sacrifice, and sacrifice is produced by the performance of prescribed duties

annād bhavanti bhūtāni - all living beings are born out of food, *parjanyād anna-sambhavaḥ* - and because of rain the food is produced. *yajñād bhavati parjanyo* - by performing *yajna*, rains happen. *yajñaḥ Karma-samudbhavaḥ* - and *yajna* itself is a result of Karma, action.

Sri Krishna tells Arjuna how existence works. Food grains grow in the agriculture fields only if rains happen on time. And the rain itself is caused by *yajna*, offering. How is rain caused by offering? There seems to be more to it than what meets the eye! In this verse, rain represents good results or prosperity.

For example, a country is ruled by a Prime Minister or President and if that Prime Minister along with his staff work with an attitude of service or *yajna*, the country will prosper. If they work with a selfish attitude, the country will be ruined. The same applies to society and people at all levels - our workplaces and homes too. Prosperity comes to us in the form of many things in life, including timely rains. This attitude of service is called Karma Yoga.

Sri Krishna tells Arjuna that all of us have to work with an attitude of service, in order to usher in prosperity to all. Whereas work done with a selfish attitude will only bring ruin - whether it is country or society or family.

annād bhavanti bhūtāni
parjanyād anna-sambhavaḥ I
yajñād bhavati parjanyo
yajñaḥ Karma-samudbhavaḥ II3.14II

****

Shloka 3.21

Whatever actions great persons perform, other people follow. Whatever standards they set, all the world pursues

Yes, whatever leaders practice, others follow. All of us practice 'follow the leader'. Whatever the leader takes as the guiding principle in his life, his followers emulate. So Sri Krishna says that leading society in the right path is the responsibility of the leaders.

Whether it is leaders in an organization or leaders in society, they set the standard. They set the standard for others to follow. That's why we say *yathā rāja, tathā prajā* – as is the king, so are the citizens. If the rulers are corrupt, society is corrupt. If the rulers are greedy, society is greedy. If the rulers are ambitious, people are ambitious. So leaders have a great responsibility to conduct themselves properly.

Who are role models for society? Film stars are role models for most people. Their fans dress, talk and even style their hair like the stars they adore. What is the motivation behind this? Film stars are famous. They have plenty of money and a lavish lifestyle. Their fans believe that if they emulate their favorite heroes or heroines, some of this luck, prosperity and charisma may knock at their doors too.

All leaders exert this kind of influence in their own spheres. Whatever the leader does, others do too. That's why Sri Krishna tells Arjuna, "O' Arjuna, you have a great responsibility. You are a leader. You should lead your army towards victory because this war is a Battle of Righteousness or *dharma yuddha*. If you yourself get depressed, how will you set the moral standard for your soldiers? All your followers will be demoralized. The results of this will be disastrous. So understand your responsibility as a leader and live up to it."

This applies to us too. Whatever we do influences those who come into contact with us. Children emulate their parents. Parents advise their children to behave in a certain way. But children don't do what their parents say. They do whatever they see their parents do.

Here's an interesting story. A father took his son to a great Master and said, "Mahatma ji, my son is eating lot of sugar. Would you please advise him to stop this?" The Master asked him to come back with his son next week. When they went to him after a week, the Master looked at the child and said, "Don't eat so much sugar, my child." The child immediately agreed. Then the father asked the Master, "Mahatma ji, you could have told him this last week itself. Why did you delay it unnecessarily?" The Master laughed and replied, "When you asked me to advise your son, I myself had the habit of eating too much sugar. Since last week I dropped this habit. Now I am eligible to ask your son to eat less sugar."

So before we advise anyone else, we should first practice it ourselves. Walk the talk. That is why Gandhiji said, "Be the change you want to see." The change should begin with you. The change should begin in every home before it can manifest in society. Be a leader and lead by example.

yad yad ācharati śhreṣhṭhas tat tad evetaro janaḥ
sa yat pramāṇaṁ kurute lokas tad anuvartate
II3.21II

****

Shloka 3.27

***The bewildered spirit soul, under the influence of
the three modes of material nature, thinks himself
to be the doer of activities, which are in actuality
carried out by nature***

prakṛiteḥ kriyamāṇāni means all actions are done by
nature; *guṇaiḥ Karmaṇi sarvaśhaḥ* means all actions
performed by three gunas of nature, three qualities of
nature that are sattva, rajō and tamō guna;
ahankāra-vimūḍhātmā kartāham iti manyate means
one who has forgotten his own nature, because of
the ego (ahankara) thinks that he is the doer. This
appears to be a very strange statement by Sri
Krishna.

In life we get tempted by seeing many things and we
tend to do a lot of things only due to the temptations.
We want to eat or we want to drink or we want to
enjoy. We act upon our desires and our samskāra.
So, desires lead us to thoughts, thoughts lead us to
action, actions force us to do something. Actions

bring fruits of action and those in turn create some more impressions.

So, who is doing something? Who is the real doer? The real doer is the impression present in our mind. There are so many impressions present in our mind. These impressions are acquired while growing up, interacting with society in various ways. They are deep rooted and these impressions give rise to desires and desires give rise to actions and actions give rise to fruits of action. So, who is the real doer? In reality the impressions within us are causing the actions, and impressions vary depending on the inner quality called guna. Three gunas are sattva, rajō and tamō guna.

A person who is sāttvik in nature will have more sātvik Impressions. He will have desires for studying scriptures, teaching and other such similar type of desires. All related to sātvik desires. A rājsik person will have the desire to act. And a tāmasik person will have a desire for laziness and enjoyment. So, all our actions are dependent on nature. 'Nature' is nothing but prakriti consisting of sattva, rajō and tamō guna. But we start thinking that we are doing the action. In reality I am not the 'Doer', I am the 'Witness'. But being identified with nature, I start thinking that I am the 'Doer', "I am the body, I am the mind and I am the Intellect".

The problem is Ignorance. Ignorance of our self-nature. We think that we are the 'doer', we think we are the 'thinker' and we think that we are the 'enjoyer'. None of this we are. It's all happening because of Prakriti or Nature. Realize yourself and become free from these Prakriti Nature.

prakṛiteḥ kriyamāṇāni guṇaiḥ Karmaṇi sarvaśhaḥ ahankāra-vimūḍhātmā kartāham iti manyate ll3.27ll

****

Shloka 3. 37

The Blessed Lord said: It is lust only, Arjuna, which is born of contact with the material modes of passion and later transformed into wrath, and which is the all-devouring, sinful enemy of this world

kāma eṣha krodha eṣha - the 'Desire' and the 'Anger' both are born out of Rajo Guna. *mahāśhano mahā-pāpmā* - this is a big fire and they cause the biggest sins. *viddhyenam iha vairiṇam* - understand that these are your enemies.

Sri Krishna speaks to Arjuna - he speaks about kāma, desire and krodha, anger. kāma and krodha both are

81

born out of the mode of nature called rajō guna. rajō guna is responsible for restlessness and activity. rajō guna is also responsible for the projection or vikshepa, the projection of non-reality. rajō guna causes desire; I see something; I want to have that. I hear about something; I like it or I dislike it. I want to taste something. Desire per se is not wrong, because some amount of desire is required for survival, for growth, but there is no end to desires. The desires keep on multiplying.

There is a story of a monk, all that he had was a pair of clothes. He was living on a mountain top, away from the world, alone, except for a rat which would chew his clothes. He is having difficulty now. So, to take care of the rat, he brings a cat. Rat is gone now but the cat has to be fed with milk, so he requires a cow. He brings a cow. To take care of the cow he gets married and to take care of the wife he starts working. He came down from the mountain, he started working in the field. Then he had children, he had to work harder, right. This way, desires keep on multiplying, there is no end to desires.

When you fulfill the desires, you feel happy, when you are not able to fulfill the desire, you feel depressed and angry. Desire and anger are the root cause of all evils. When the desire can be fulfilled in the rightful way, life will be alright, it will be peaceful. But many times, there are desires which are beyond your means, for which people start getting out of the legal system. They start getting into petty crimes or violation of human behavior, so then what happens? They get into the wrong side of the law, either moral law or divine law of Karma. On the other hand, if they don't get what they want, they start getting angry. In anger people forget themselves and they start doing things which are unimaginable and horrible. They may hurt others, hit others or they may even kill. Some people throw whatever is in their hand. Once somebody had bought a nice and expensive watch. In the fit of temper, he threw the watch and it broke and later he realized the mistake and regretted it. So they start regretting only after the anger subsides.

For desire people do something, for anger people do something that they should have not done. So their 'anger' and 'desire' makes them sin. They cause great sins. They are the source of sins in human beings. They are like fire, once expressed the desire will never end. One desire will lead to another, another desire will lead to one another and get into endless cycles of desires. It's like pouring ghee into the fire. The ghee makes the fire burn more. Anger is also like fire. In the fit of temper, they hurt somebody and that person starts taking revenge and this will lead to bad relationships, damaged relationships.

Now this is about expression. But if you suppress desire and anger what will happen? They will go into the sub-conscious. They will be alive there, they will find another opportunity to come out. Somebody has a desire for smoking, he suppresses the desire for smoking, then he will start chewing paan. It expresses itself in some other way. Anger, if suppressed, will start burning. Have you heard of the heartburn, stomach burn? These are suppressed emotions.

Suppressed emotions hurt the body. Whether you express or suppress, they burn like fire. These are the big enemies of human beings. You should learn how to go beyond expression and suppression. That's called 'sublimation'. That's the art of yoga, that's the art of meditation, to go beyond both anger and desire. It's not dropping or it's not suppressing or it's not expressing, just going beyond.
In our country there is a great amount of respect given to somebody who has mastered this 'anger' and 'desire'. Such people are called Mahaveera.

The title Mahaveera means a great warrior. In many other countries warrior is one who has killed many enemies, whereas in India, a great warrior is one who has killed his enemies of 'anger' and 'desire'. Buddhist call such a person as Arhat/Arahant. Arhat spilt as ari hanta - ari means enemies, hanta means destroyer. Somebody who has destroyed his enemies called anger and desire is qualified to be called Arahant, these are enlightened beings.

Sri Krishna tells Arjuna to go beyond 'anger' and 'desire', be free from these enemies. May all of us contemplate on this truth, go beyond anger and desire and attain peaceful living.

sri bhagavān uvācha
kāma eṣha krodha eṣha
rajo-guṇa-samudbhavaḥ I
mahāśhano mahā-pāpmā
viddhyenam iha vairiṇam II3.37II

****

CHAPTER 4: JNĀNA KARMA SANYĀSA YOGA

Shloka 4.1

The Blessed Lord said:
I instructed this imperishable science of yoga to the sun-god, Vivasvan, and Vivasvan instructed it to Manu, the father of mankind, and Manu in turn instructed it to Iksvaku.

The fourth chapter of Bhagavad Gita is titled 'Jnāna Karma Sanyāsa Yoga'. The third chapter was called Karma Yoga, meaning to drop the desire for the fruits of actions. Jnāna Karma Sanyāsa Yoga. is to drop the doer-ship. By dropping the doer-ship, you are not stopping the work. By dropping the identification of yourself as the doer and realizing that you are a pure witness and not a doer, you become free from Karma and this can happen only throughJnāna. That is why it is 'Jnāna Karma Sanyāsa Yoga'.

Sri Krishna tells Arjuna, this yoga which is imperishable, he gave it to Surya, the Sun God. Vivasvān the Sun God gave it to Manu Chakravarty, who is the originator of the human race (the English word 'man' comes from here). Manu in turn told this to Iksvāku, the emperor. This is the tradition of this teaching. Bhagavān gives confidence to Arjuna that the advice being given to him is not a randomly picked or a cooked up one. Whereas there is a tradition of *guru-shishya parampara* from where it originates. Whatever is being taught has an ancient tradition associated with it. From time immemorial people have been practicing this Yoga and passing it on to the next generations. What is valuable always gets passed on from one generation to another generation.

Here the knowledge has been transmitted from one emperor - Manu, to another - Iksvāku - both mighty and powerful people. When the rulers of a country get wisdom, all the people of the country will benefit. If the rulers themselves don't have wisdom, then what wisdom can people have.

So, the wisdom of ātmajnāna or Self-knowledge, wisdom ofJnāna Karma Sanyāsa Yoga is an ancient science, passed on Bhagavān to Surya to Manu to Iksvāku. This is not only in the case of ātmajnāna, we have seen how a mother teaches cooking to her daughter to make a variety of dishes. Making a delicacy dish is not easy, you need to add sugar/salt and various ingredients in the right proportion, that has to be taught by somebody. A mother would have taught that to her daughter, daughter will teach that in turn to her daughter. Likewise, even a simple skill like cooking has to be passed on from generation to generation. Otherwise, that knowledge/method of cooking will get lost.

Then what to say about knowledge of the Self? It has to be passed on from generation to generation in an unbroken tradition. This pure wisdom has to be passed on. Sri Krishna is the originator of this wisdom and from there it got passed on to many kings, many people have been benefited from this knowledge. Sri Krishna says I am not going to teach you something new, I am going to teach you ancient wisdom. It is time to teach the wisdom, it has been proved to be valuable to many kings and emperors, that will benefit you also, O' Arjuna.

sri bhagavān uvācha
imaṁ vivasvate yogaṁ
proktavān aham avyayam I
vivasvān manave prāha
manur ikṣhvākave 'bravīt
II4.1II

****

Shloka 4.2

O Arjuna, subduer of enemies, the saintly kings received this science of Yoga through a

A lamp can light many lamps. Similarly, the wisdom of an enlightened Master can light up many lives. In earlier times, Masters established schooling systems called Gurukulas for passing on wisdom, which was transmitted from one generation to the other through a chain of Master-disciple relationship called Guru parampara. There are examples of enlightened royal sages like Maharaja Janaka receiving wisdom from Master Ashtavakra and passing on the wisdom to many more seekers.

ātma vichara has thus been passed from one generation to the next. Why did the ancient sages initiate the kings into this knowledge? They were very wise - they did that because the kings in turn could set up systems to pass it on to their citizens. For instance, King Ashoka who was transformed by Bhagavān Buddha's teachings of love, peace and compassion, made it his mission to spread this knowledge not only in India, but in many of the nearby countries like Sri Lanka and Afghanistan. So, there were many wise kings even before King Ashoka who set up education systems that revolved around ātma vichara. Therefore the wisdom of the sages was accessible to everyone.

However, somewhere along the line this chain of tradition was broken. There were many reasons for this – natural calamities, wars, invaders who did their best to corrupt this tradition. There could have been a dearth of knowledgeable teachers and willing students. Due to the convergence of many factors, the system of knowledge transmission was disrupted. Sri Krishna is telling Arjuna that the reason he had not heard of the science of Yoga is because of this disruption. But Arjuna is now receiving this wisdom directly from Sri Krishna himself.

evaṁ paramparā-prāptam imaṁ rājarṣhayo viduḥ
sa kāleneha mahatā yogo naṣhṭaḥ parantapa
II4.2II

****

Shloka 4.3

That very ancient science of the relationship with the Supreme is today told by me to you because you are my devotee as well as my friend; therefore you can understand the transcendental mystery of this science

Krishna said, "O' Arjuna, you are my closest friend and also my devotee, that's why I am telling you the secret. This ancient Yoga which has been kept as a secret is now revealed to you". The Yoga of Self-Knowledge or Self-Realization is a secret. Is this a secret like those industry secrets which you get patented?. Is it a secret like a military secret or some personal information? No, it is a secret because not many people want to know it, and many are not interested in this knowledge either. This is a knowledge which can be given to only those who seek. It's not useful for those who don't seek. And even if they listen, they will not understand, because of lack of interest. That's why this knowledge remains secret.

This secret knowledge has been told by Sri Krishna to Arjuna. Why? Because Arjuna is a friend, Arjuna is a devotee. Friends keep talking for hours together and they talk about the deepest secrets in their heart. So, this secret of Self Knowledge, Krishna tells Arjuna because he is not only a friend, but also a great devotee of Krishna.

But Self Knowledge (ātma jnāna) is not a subject that two friends can discuss like any other subject. ātmaJnāna has to come from an Enlightened Master to a disciple. This knowledge has to come from an authorized source, the right source.

For example, a person who has a stomach ache can take the medicine recommended by his friend, but the pain may still persist because that friend is not a doctor. But when he takes the medicine prescribed by the doctor, his stomach ache will disappear.

Similarly, ātma jnāna is a subject which has to be taught by a realized master. Krishna shares this secret with Arjuna, because Arjuna has accepted Sri Krishna as a realized master and surrendered to him. Arjuna being a friend and a disciple, is now a worthy recipient of this knowledge. That's what Sri Krishna says.

sa evāyaṁ mayā te 'dya
 yogaḥ proktaḥ purātanaḥ I
Bhakto 'si me sakhā cheti
rahasyaṁ hyetad uttamam II4.3II

****

Shloka 4.6

Although I am unborn and My transcendental body never deteriorates, and although I am the Lord of all sentient beings, I still appear in every millennium in My original transcendental form

ajo 'pi sann avyayatma - I am birthless, I am the Master of all living beings.

bhutanam isvaro 'pi san - Even then, I control the prakriti (nature) and take birth with my Maya. This is the message of Sri Krishna.

Sri Krishna is Paramātma. *ātma* is birthless and deathless. *ātma*, the Consciousness is the eternal principle. That eternal principle creates a body for manifestation in this world and enters into the body for taking care of the righteousness, upholding the righteousness - Dharma. This is called an avatāra.

Sri Krishna tells Arjuna that the ancient tradition of spiritual knowledge got lost at various points of time. But the Lord takes the responsibility of restoring it and the Lord himself has to come to restore it. The Lord takes the form of a human body to take that knowledge to people and bring the wisdom back in the society. This is called incarnation or *avatāra*.

One day, Akbar asked Birbal, "I have heard that Bhagavān takes *avatāra*, Bhagavān takes the human form. How is it possible?" Birbal says, "Yes, it is very much possible. I will demonstrate to you". One day the two of them were walking near a lake and Akbar's son was boating in that lake. Suddenly, he fell into the water. Seeing that, Akbar immediately jumped into the water and tried rescuing the boy, but he saw that it was not his son, but a doll. A doll looking like Akbar's son had been made and pushed into water.

Akbar got angry at Birbal and started shouting at him, he said, "How dare you play this prank on me?" Birbal replied, "Maharaj, why did you jump into the water? You could have called your servants". Akbar replied, "How can I do that? It is my son who fell into the water."

Birbal said, "Similarly for Bhagavān, all of us on earth are his children. When there is *ajnāna*, *adharma* and when the Self Knowledge is lost, there will be chaos in the society. Unrighteousness will rule the day. People will be in trouble. That's when Lord himself comes in the form of a human being to uphold Dharma. He doesn't wait for someone else or send his servants. He himself will come in the human form to uphold Dharma. That is called an *avatāra*. It is the grace of the Lord that this sacred teaching of ātma jnāna is available to human kind all the time and whenever it is lost, Bhagavān himself takes the form to restore Dharma.

ajo 'pi sann avyayatma
bhutanam isvaro 'pi san I
prakrtim svam adhisthaya
sambhavamy atma-mayaya II4.6II

****

Shloka 4.7, 4.8

Whenever there is a decline in righteousness and an increase in unrighteousness, O Arjuna, at that time I manifest Myself on earth (4.7)

*In order to deliver the pious and to annihilate the miscreants, as well as to reestablish the principles of religion, I advent Myself millennium after millennium (4.8)***

paritrānayā sādhunām - To protect the good people
vinasaya ca duskrtām - To destroy the evil doers. And
dharma-samsthāpanārthāya - To establish the righteousness
sambhavāmi yuge yuge - I will take birth again and again and again, again to upholdDharma.

We have to be very grateful to the Lord, Bhagavān. He takes human birth, even though he has no need to take it. He goes through human life to teach human beings, to show human beings the path ofDharma, path of righteousness.

What is this Dharma? Dharma is not religion. Dharma has no religion, it is wrongly translated as religion. *dhārayati itiDharmah*. One which upholds and protects is calledDharma. What does it protect? The universal laws and the universal principles which protect human beings is calledDharma. At various levels of existence there are principles operating. At the macro level, at the galactic level there is movement of stars, galaxies, a very orderly movement and this orderly movement is calledDharma.

At the earthly level, there is an orderly change in the weather pattern... summer, winter, and there is a rainy season. All these follow a certain pattern to ensure that life is sustained. There is an order in our body, the biological order. Our heart beats properly, lungs operate, eyes operate, brain operates in an orderly manner. Also at microcosmic level, there is an order. Atoms, electrons, neutros etc move with precision. There is order in this universe, otherwise it would have been chaotic. This order is calledDharma.

Sometimes Dharma gets lost, but not in the macrocosmic order, in the microcosmic order or in the human body. Dharma gets lost in the human mind. Whenever a human being performs actions in accordance with universal laws, it becomesDharma. Whenever he goes against the universal laws, it becomes Karma. Following universal laws isDharma but human beings don't follow. They think that there is nobody to oversee this order. Instead of following what is right, they think that whatever they do is right. They don't know that they don't have any understanding of these Universal Principles. And why do they go on the path of Adharma? Because of the lack of Self Knowledge, *atma jnāna.* They live in ignorance and hence there is unrighteousness or *adharma*. When we have ātmaJnāna, there will be no place for *adharma*.

Sri Krishna already said that the wisdom got lost because the chain of passing on this sacred knowledge from one generation to another got broken. There were no right recipients or right masters. So, whenever there is disorder, then Bhagavān himself takes the human form to uphold Dharma. Upholding Dharma means giving right wisdom, the right knowledge by doing which Dharma is restored. In the process, he will destroy those who are those who are evil doers. And he will protect the good-natured ones who follow Dharma.

He also punishes the evil-doers, playing the role of a policeman. Dharma can be compared to a universal law and order. Just like there is a local law and order in any country, there is a Universal Law and order. In a country, we have to follow law and order, else there will be chaos everywhere. For example, if anyone violates traffic rules, the traffic cop will punish them and this is exactly what Sri Krishna does. He is the universal policeman. If anyone violates the universal law and order, he will come down to earth as a human being and punish them. Also, he helps people who are following Dharma to move forward in life.

This is the message of Bhagavān. We have to be grateful to Bhagavan for the grace being showered on us in the form of his teaching - Bhagavad Gita. May all of us follow this teaching, purify ourselves and follow the path of Dharma.

yadā yadā hi dharmasya
glānir bhavati bhārata I
abhyutthānam adharmasya
tadātmānaṁ sṛijāmyaham II4.7II

paritrāṇāya sādhūnāṁ
vināśhāya cha duṣhkṛitām I
dharma-sansthāpanārthāya
sambhavāmi yuge yuge II4.8II

****

Shloka 4.9

One who knows the transcendental nature of My appearance and activities does not, upon leaving the body, take his birth again in this material world, but attains My eternal abode, O' Arjuna!

tyaktva deham - " After dropping the body, he will not take birth again. He will attain me only Arjuna". Sri Krishna says, "O' Arjuna, if you understand my birth and my action, you will be free from bondage of birth and death." Very strange! If I understand my birth and my actions, I may be free from my birth and death. But Sri Krishna says you have to understand the birth and actions of the Lord to be free from your birth and death. Why so?

There is a difference between the birth of the Lord and the birth of human beings. Bhagavān takes birth to upholdDharma. His birth is for Dharma whereas ordinary human beings' birth is for Karma. Bhagavān has a choice in taking the right type of body and right type of place for upholding Dharma. Whereas we don't have a choice because we are driven by the force of karmic impressions. Our karmic impressions, the last impressions at the time of death will take us to another place, another birth. We cannot escape that. Our choices are limited because of the karmic load we have. So there is a difference between the birth of the Lord and the birth of a human being.

There is a difference between the action of the Lord and actions of human beings. All the actions of Bhagavān are for *loka kalyāna* - welfare of the world, for uplifting society, for establishing Dharma. Whereas human being's actions are for fulfillment of their desires, selfish in nature. Selfish actions will bring more Karma. Whereas Bhagavān is born not because of Karma, He is born for Dharma   -

righteousness. His actions are all for unselfish reasons, for upholding Dharma in society.

If we understand the difference between our birth and the birth of the Lord, the difference between our actions and the actions of the Lord, then we will become free. Because, we understand that, to be free from birth and death cycle one has to be free from Karma. To be free from Karma, we have to follow Dharma. Follow the Lord means, follow the way the Lord acts, follow the way Bhagavān carries out his responsibilities in the world. All his actions are for the welfare of the world. Similarly, if we follow the Lord, perform our actions in a very unselfish way, if we perform Karma Yoga, we will be free from karmic bondage while alive, then we will not be entering into the circle of birth and death. You will be free from the cycle of birth and death.

janma Karma cha me divyam
evaṁ yo vetti tattvataḥ I
tyaktvā dehaṁ punar janma
naiti mām eti so 'rjuna II4.9II

****

Shloka 4.10

Being free from attachment, fear and anger, becoming fully absorbed in Me, and taking refuge in Me, many persons in the past became purified by knowledge of Me, and thus attained My divine love

Attachment is expressed as attraction and repulsion. How do we become free from attraction and repulsion? How do we drop fear and anger? In an earlier shloka Sri Krishna revealed that desire is the root cause of fear, anger, attraction and repulsion. Let's see if that is true according to our own experience. I have a desire to acquire a car. Whenever I see the model I favor, I experience a pull of attraction towards it. If I see models I don't like, I feel repelled by them. I start saving money to buy the car, but I'm afraid that I may never have enough money. I'm apprehensive that the particular model I want may become obsolete before I can afford it. After all that effort, if I can't buy the car, I get angry. If I do buy the car, I'm thrilled, but the happiness lasts only for a short while. So, even when we analyze our own experience, we see that desire is indeed the root cause of fear, anger, attraction and repulsion.

Then should we live without any desires? No, it is very difficult to live without desires. Moreover, desire can be a powerful ally if used correctly. Recognising this, our sages asked us to direct the force of desire towards God. When we develop a desire to attain God, we become free from all other desires. A higher desire helps us to drop all lower ones. We see this in the lives of achievers too. When an athlete is passionate about qualifying for the Olympics, he drops most of his other pastimes. To run a race of a few seconds, he trains for years. He disciplines himself by waking up early to practice. He cuts down on entertainment time and eats only healthy food. He doesn't mind doing all this because of his passionate desire to run in the Olympics. We also see rank holders in academics having the same focus on their studies.

In our own lives we have experienced that higher desires replace lower ones many times. Each time we have achieved something worthwhile in life, we have followed this process. So don't waste time in trying to suppress or drop desires. Instead, hold on passionately to a higher desire. Then the lower ones drop away on their own like dry leaves that fall from a tree. This is the path all devotees follow. They only yearn to see God. So they are freed from attraction, repulsion, fear and anger. They say, "Lord, I depend only on you. I accept whatever you give me as *prasādam*." They surrender to the Lord and become free. If we focus on Self Realization and make it our first priority in life, we too will be free from attraction, repulsion, fear and anger.

***Vīta-rāga-bhaya-krodhā
man-mayā mām upāSritāḥ I
bahavo jnāna-tapasā pūtā
mad-bhāvam āgatāḥ II4.10II***

****

Shloka 4.11

In whatever way people surrender unto Me, I reciprocate accordingly. Everyone follows My path, knowingly or unknowingly, O' son of Pritha

All of us have our own way of approaching things, our own tastes, likes and dislikes. No two people are alike. Therefore there are also many ways of worshiping the Supreme Being. Depending on our temperament, we relate to God in different ways.

Those who are action oriented follow the path of Karma Yoga. They surrender the fruits of their actions to God and accept the outcome as his prasadam or grace. They are called Karma Yogis. Those with a devotional temperament worship God using rituals. They are always immersed in thoughts of adoration and meditation. They are devotees or bhaktas.

Many work on the pranic energy in the body to achieve higher levels of consciousness. We call them kriya Yogis.Jnāna Yogis contemplate on spiritual truths in the Upanishads and attain the highest wisdom.

Though people approach God through such different paths, God showers his grace upon them all like the Sun who lights up all things on earth. The Sun does not show any partiality. Sunlight falls equally on rocks, rivers, plants, animals, sinners and saints. Similarly the Lord is impartial and bestows his grace on all spiritual aspirants or sadhakas. He connects to them through the form they adore and grants them success in their own paths. But all of us may not understand this. We often think that our way is superior and the way in which we relate to God is the best way. This creates a lot of unnecessary friction and turmoil in society. Children address their mother in different ways, but she loves all of them equally and responds to each one of them in a special way. In the same way the Lord says, "Each one of you is dear to me. Follow any path that appeals to you. All of them lead to me."

ye yatha mam prapadyante
tams tathaiva bhajamy aham I
mama vartmanuvartante
manusyah partha sarvasah II4.11II

****

Shloka 4.13

The four categories of occupations were created by Me according to people's qualities and activities. Although I am the Creator of this system, know Me to be the Non-doer and Eternal

What are the four occupations or categories that Sri Krishna speaks of in this shloka? They are *brahmana, kshatriya, vaishya and shudra.* Unfortunately in India these are now regarded as iron clad castes that are conferred upon us by birth. But this was not the original way the varnashrama system was set up. The Lord said that the inborn tendencies of each human being decide what kind of occupation they will take up in life. By birth, we have certain tendencies or samskaras which we carry over from our past lives. They color the way we perceive life. They define the way we think, talk, behave and act. They manifest as skills, talents and aptitudes. If we take up professions where we can exercise these aptitudes, we are sure to excel in them.

When someone has a desire for higher learning and wants to realize the true nature of the universe, God or his own Self, he is called a *brahmana*. If he probes into the laws that govern creation, he becomes a scientist. On the other hand if he seeks to understand his own true nature, he becomes an enlightened person or Jnāni. Seeking knowledge is the inner urge of a *brahmana*.

A *kshatriya* has a desire to acquire power and rule the country. That is why we say *kshinanām trayate iti kshatriyah* – the one who uses his power to protect the weak is a *kshatriya*. When someone has this tendency, he will gravitate into administration or governance. A *vaishya* is one who has a natural flair for business. He is a good investor who creates jobs and generates wealth. He may also come up with strategies to generate surplus income to use for charity. Who is a *shudra*? There is a saying *shuchanat drava iti shudrah* – the one who melts at the sight of suffering is a *shudra*. He rushes to help others and engages himself in service. So these are the four main categories of human beings based on their inborn tendencies.

When the aptitude or guna and profession or Karma are well matched that person shines in life and becomes a beautiful being. When they conflict with each other, the professional performance is lacking in merit. As we discussed earlier, the caste system that is in vogue in India today bears no relationship to the varnashrama followed in ancient times. Unlike caste, varna is not conferred at birth. For instance, a child born in a doctor's family cannot become a doctor automatically. He has to study medicine and earn his doctor's degree. A politician's son cannot be a politician by birth. He has to develop the traits that are necessary for this.

Unless we learn how to manifest our qualities through our actions, they remain dormant. We should use our aptitudes for the welfare of society as well as for earning our own livelihood. This is the essence of the varnashrama system.

Even today, if we look at society, we notice this natural division of labor. The thinker class are primarily involved in intellectual pursuits. They are teachers, scientists and researchers. In the ruling class we have IAS officers, politicians and institutional heads. In the business class we have financiers, investors and entrepreneurs. We have the irreplaceable working class who maintain upkeep of society. It is unfair to put someone who has a natural flair for intellectual pursuits into administration - he may fail at that job. He shines in occupations where he can use his innate potential.

We have these four categories of people in society. Is there a common formula that can make them brilliant in their chosen occupations? Yes, if they offer every act of theirs to God, their work gets recognition and they also evolve spiritually. Karma Yoga uplifts all those who engage in it. God created these four categories of human beings for the welfare of society. It is pointless to ask, "God, why did you place me in this particular category and not another?" There is a saying *janmati jāyate shudrah* – at birth everyone is a *shudra*. All of us are innately compassionate by nature. This love and empathy should be expressed through the profession we choose based on our other aptitudes. Though God created the *varnashrama,* he has no taint of doer-ship attached to him. It is a spontaneous expression of his compassion for humanity with no expectations. God is infinite and eternal. He can never be trapped or limited by the law of Karma that governs those who identify with the body-mind-intellect complex.

catur-varnyam maya srstam
Guna-Karma-vibhagasah I
tasya kartaram api mam
viddhy akartaram avyayam II4.13II

****

Shloka 4.34

Learn the Truth by approaching a spiritual master. Inquire from him with reverence and render service unto him. Such an enlightened Saint can

***impart knowledge unto you because he has seen
the Truth***

When we perform any task, there are two things all of
us assume. We may or may not say anything about
them, but they are always present in our minds.
What are these two things? We think, "I am doing
this task." This is called doer-ship or *kartrtva.* We
also feel, "I must enjoy the result of this action." This
feeling is called enjoyer-ship or *bhoktrtva.*

These can lead to a lot of suffering. When people
don't recognise or praise our actions we feel
frustrated. If we don't get the result we expect from
our action we are disappointed. So if we want to exit
the cycle of suffering, we must drop both doer-ship
and enjoyer-ship. This is called Jnāna Karma
Sanyasa Yoga, which is the name of the chapter we
are discussing right now. In Karma Yoga we
understand that if we offer every action to the Lord
and receive its outcome as His grace or *prasādam,*
we are freed from the oscillation between joy and
disappointment caused by the successful or
unsuccessful result of our action. We accept
whatever outcome we receive as the grace of God.
So we drop the concept of being the enjoyer.

However, as we evolve, we also have to drop the
concept of, "I am the doer of this action." Without

consciousness powering the body, mind and intellect, we can do nothing. Though we know this, discarding doer-ship can be very challenging because it has become a habit with us. So many doubts arise in us about how to implement this. To clarify these doubts we need a realized Master or Jnāni.

Who is a Jnāni? He need not be a great orator. He may not be able to recite the scriptures from memory. But he has realized the truths explained in the scriptures. He is established in his true nature and exudes joy, peace and compassion all the time. He can explain the truth to us in a way that we can relate to. For instance, Sri Ramakrishna was not a scholar, but he was the living embodiment of truth. He guided hundreds of disciples on the spiritual path. Great scholars would come to him to clarify their doubts.

So it's a Jnāni alone who can impart wisdom. We will be able to receive his wisdom when we surrender to him and ask him deep, probing questions about the truth. If we ask questions merely to show that we know a lot or to test whether the Jnāni is knowledgeable, it does not qualify as deep questioning. Only when we surrender and place our burning questions before him does the Jnāni instruct

us in Self Knowledge or ātma jnāna. Sri Krishna
affirms that this is the process of acquiring wisdom.

tad viddhi praṇipātena
paripraśhnena sevayā I
upadekṣhyanti te jnānaṁ
jnāninas tattva-darśhinaḥ II4.34II

****

CHAPTER 5: KARMA SANYĀSA YOGA

Shloka 5.18

The truly learned, with the eyes of divine knowledge, see with equal vision a Brahmin, a cow, an elephant, a dog, and a dog-eater

Society has different yardsticks for different creatures. For instance, a cow is worshiped, regarded as holy while a dog may be stoned and chased away. A learned man or brahmana may be respected, but a dog eater may be treated as an outcast. An elephant may be regarded with awe for its strength and size. This is the way of society. However an enlightened being or Jnāni looks at the world in a different way. He does not discriminate based on size and strength. Nor does he differentiate based on birth, religion or caste. He realizes the divinity that is inherent in each living being and in insentient objects too. He has deep love for the whole of creation. He sees everyone with unbiased eyes.

When we identify with our body, mind and intellect, we feel that everyone is different from us. So we begin to like or dislike others based on their physical or mental characteristics. We may like people who are handsome and dislike those who are ugly. We may mingle with those we consider intelligent and shun those who seem dull. The enlightened one is a maha-ātma, a great being.   He identifies only with the Self which is also the inner Self of all.

An anecdote from Sri Ramakrishna's life illustrates this beautifully. Someone asked him to describe the essence of the Bhagavad Gita. He said, "If you go on repeating Gita, Gita, Gita…continuously, it sounds like Tyagi, Tyagi, Tyagi… Gita means song while Tyagi means to drop.   Drop what? Drop your identity of I am the body-mind-intellect and remain as the Self which you really are.

The one who has accomplished this sees the Divine in everyone. Does that mean that he treats a dog and a scholar alike? Will he allow a street dog to come in and sit on a chair next to a scholar? No, the fact that he respects each being equally does not mean that he metes out the same treatment to them. Though he sees the divinity in a lion, he is not going to bow down before it. If he does, it will eat him. He reveres it from afar and maintains his distance. On the other hand, he bows down to the feet of a scholar to express deep respect for his learning.   He has abiding love for all, but treats beings in the way they expect. Such is the wisdom of a Jnāni.

vidya-vinaya-sampanne
brahmane gavi hastini
suni caiva sva-pake ca
panditah sama-darsinah ||5.18||

****

Shloka 5.22

An intelligent person (Jnāni) does not take part in the sources of misery, which are due to contact with the material senses. O son of Kunti, such pleasures have a beginning and an end, and so the wise man does not delight in them

ye hi sansparśha-jā bhogā duḥkha-yonaya eva te
ādyantavantaḥ kaunteya na teṣhu ramate budhaḥ
sansparśha-jā bhogā - the enjoyment derived by the contact of sense organs
duḥkha-yonaya - the cause of suffering
ādyantavantaḥ - the joy is limited in nature, for a short duration and they cause suffering
na teṣhu ramate budhaḥ - that's why the real ones, the Jnānis, don't derive pleasure from sense organs

We have five sense organs through which we experience the world - sight with eyes, sound with ears, taste through the tongue, smell with the nose and touch or feeling via skin. So the *ajnāni*, one who sees this world through the senses, gets attracted with the objects of the senses. Something looks beautiful and he wants to pursue that. Something feels good, he wants to have that. So, this pursuit of sense organs is for deriving joy from sense organs i.e. sensations. Is it good, is it long lasting? Any joy derived from sense organs is temporary in nature, momentary. For example, like sweets, we can taste only a little bit of sweet - it is temporary in nature, it is not permanent. But because we enjoy it a little bit, we become addicted to that sensation. We wish to have more and more of that sweet experience, and probably land up being diabetic. This is the case with any sense organ.

The Jnāni is one who has become free from this temptation, not because he discards them but because he has found much more meaning or much more joy within himself. That's why four categories of beings are seen.

bhogi means one who is after sense enjoyment i.e. enjoyment of objects of sense organs. He constantly searches for objects of sense organs. A person who is a *bhogi*, constantly enjoying sense objects, becomes a rogi, the diseased person. If somebody likes liquor and keeps indulging in it, the liver is bound to get affected - he becomes a *rogi*.

Somebody who realizes that the addiction to objects of sense organs is dangerous but can be happy without the external addiction is called a Yogi. He meditates or practices pranayama regularly to get the bliss within himself.

There is another category of person who has realized that he is of the nature of bliss. He is called a Jnāni. So the four categories are: *bhogi, rogi,* Yogi and Jnāni. The Jnāni is a realized person. He is always blissful. He doesn't need any objects to indulge his sense organs. He is always blissful. That doesn't mean that he doesn't drink, or eat or enjoy the world, but his focus and purpose are different.

So, the *ajnāni* acts to get bliss out of objects of the senses, while the Jnāni acts out of bliss. For bliss and out of bliss - that's the difference between a Jnāni and an *ajnāni*!

ye hi sansparśha-jā bhogā
duḥkha-yonaya eva te I
ādyantavantaḥ kaunteya
na teṣhu ramate budhaḥ II5.22II

****

Shloka 5.29

Having realized Me as the enjoyer of all sacrifices and austerities, the Supreme Lord of all the worlds and the selfless friend of all living beings, My devotee attains peace

bhoktāraṁ yajña-tapasāṁ- the Yogi understands that bhagwan the lord is the enjoyer of fruits of both action and penance. He is the lord of universe, *sarva-loka-maheśhvaram,* and he is compassionate to all living beings, *suhṛidaṁ sarva-bhūtānāṁ.* This is the understanding of Yogi and therefore he attains peace.

People undertake different types of spiritual practices. Some people do *yajna*, a service as an offering to lord. When we do service, we should have the attitude of serving the lord, not for the human being or anybody. Different kinds of yajna are performed - *bhuta yajna, pitru yajna, manusya yajna, deva yajna, rishi yajna.*

bhuta yajna means compassion to all living beings, all animals, when you are compassionate to all animals, in reality we are actually offering our respect to the divine in that animal. God is there in all living beings; we are offering our respect to that. With that attitude when we do, the Lord is the one who enjoys our service. He receives our service and gives fruits of that. He is the *yajna-phala-dāta* - he blesses us.

Similarly, when you do service to human beings, actually it is service to the lord in human beings, *nara-nārāyana* seva, service to the lord, lord will be pleased. And he will bless us. If you think that we are doing service to a person, spiritual attainment may not happen. Swami Vivekananda went to Chicago in America and there are many people very thoroughly impressed by his speeches. They came and paid respect to Vivekananda. One rich man came and gave 5000 dollars to Vivekananda. Vivekananda kept the cheque inside his pocket. The man was furious, Swami Vivekananda didn't say thanks. Vivekananda smiled and said, 'it is you who have to thank me, becauseI am giving you an opportunity to serve the poor'.

It's not the poor who we are serving, it's the lord in the human being, lord in the poor whom we are offering our respect to. You have to be thankful for that. The attitude of service yajna for all of us is that. When you do service, it is the lord who receives the service.

tapas when penance, different types of penance, penance means taming the mind and body, purifying the mind and body. External penance like weightlifting   is a physical act, whereas internal penance is done for purification of *vasanās*, impressions and attaining the lord.This penance is for attaining lord, that lord is the recipient, or lord is the destination of penance.

sarva-bhuta-maheśhvaram - he is lord of all living beings, and he is compassionate and loving to all living beings. He has no partiality to anybody, he is compassionate towards all living beings. Like a mother, he treats all children, all of creation, all living beings equally. But by doing penance or yajna you become purer, so more dignity shines through you. It's not that the lord becomes partial towards you. So, this is the understanding of Yogi. That's why he puts in self-effort to purify himself and become closer to lord and he attains peace in the process.

bhoktāraṁ yajña-tapasāṁ
sarva-loka-maheśhvaram I
suhṛidaṁ sarva-bhūtānāṁ jñātvā
māṁ śhāntim ṛichchhati II5.29II

****

CHAPTER 6: DHYĀNA YOGA

Introduction

Chapter 6 of the Bhagavad Gita is titled Dhyāna Yoga which means Yoga of Meditation. In this chapter, Sri Krishna talks about the process of meditation, taking mind inwards, meditating on the Self and realizing the Self. This chapter logically follows the previous chapters.

Chapter 3 of the Gita outlined Karma Yoga, the Yoga of Action in which Sri Krishna taught that work should become worship, an offering to the lord. Any fruits of actions which may come should be accepted with equanimity, as blessings from the divine. When you convert your work as worship to God, we will work more efficiently without getting distracted by any hurdles or expectation of results. Hence, none of our actions will leave any impressions in our mind. This is the objective of Karma Yoga - to set us free from the effects and results of action. In this process we drop the concept of bhokta, or enjoyer. The idea, "I am the enjoyer or victim of fruits of action" is dropped. A Karma Yogi will say, "I am blissful all the time because bliss is within me. My happiness is not dependent on the results of my actions, and I will not be depressed if results are not in my favor". The *bhoktrtva* (enjoyership) is dropped in Karma Yoga.

Then comes the next concept in chapter 4 where Sri Krishna outlines Jnāna Karma Sanyāsa Yoga where the concept of doership is dropped through Jnāna. As we start realizing the way this universe works, we will understand that we are not the doer, and actions are happening because of the material nature - prakriti. So I am Self, not the doer, karta, and not affected by the action. Thus the concept of doership - *kartrtva* - is dropped with Jnāna.

After dropping enjoyership and doership, a stage will come where one drops the action also. All selfish actions and ego-centric actions are dropped. And that person lives only for the sake of service for the welfare of the universe. This is the real meaning of *sanyāsa* or renunciation of action itself. It doesn't mean that a *sanyāsi* will not act at all. On the other hand, he acts for the welfare of the world. No selfish actions are involved, this is called real *sanyāsa*.

So, with these different types ofYogas discussed in chapters 3, 4, 5, our mind is purified, it becomes very silent and we are ready for meditation, the inward journey of the mind. And when the mind is purified through Karma Yoga and Sanyāsa Yoga, it can be withdrawn to be established in the Self. This is called Dhyāna Yoga, chapter 6. Let's study Dhyāna Yoga.

Shloka 6.1

The Supreme Lord said: Those who perform prescribed duties without desiring the results of their actions are actual sanyāsīs (renunciates) and Yogis, not those who have merely ceased performing sacrifices such as agnihotra yajna or abandoned physical activities

We have different concepts of who is an ascetic or a Yogi. We recognise ascetics through their ochre robes or monasteries. So also we say someone is a Yogi if he is engaged in practicing Yogic postures or other external characteristics like austere lifestyle, simple dress, long matted locks and so on.

However Sri Krishna says, "External characteristics alone do not define an ascetic or Yogi. What is more important is his internal state. If a person is performing his duties without any attachment to the results, then he is a true Karma Yogi. He may not have renounced his home and hearth, but he has dropped doer-ship and enjoyer-ship. He is not a *karta* or *bhokta* – doer or enjoyer. This is what an ascetic is trying to reach by renouncing his home, family and profession. This is what a Yogi is trying to attain by practicing Yoga."

In bygone days a householder or *grihastha* would perform an obligatory fire ritual called *agnihotra* every day. But anyone who became a monk would stop performing this ritual. This was one of the characteristics of a monk. But here Sri Krishna draws our attention to a remarkable truth. It is not the external way of living that matters, it is always our internal state that is of paramount importance.

sri bhagavān uvācha,
anāSritaḥ Karma-phalaṁ
kāryaṁ Karma karoti yaḥ I
sa sannyāsī cha Yogi cha
na niragnir na chākriyaḥ II6.1II

****

Shloka 6.3

To the soul who is aspiring for perfection in Yoga, work without attachment is said to be the means; to the Sage who is already elevated in Yoga, tranquility in meditation is said to be the means

Most of us have innumerable desires and ambitions. So the mind gets distracted by sense objects and we keep thinking, "I want this, I want that..." So the energies of the mind are always scattered.   It is impossible for a scattered mind to focus on meditation. That is why Sri Krishna says, "For such a person, the first step is *nishkāma Karma*. His work has to become worship. He has to perform each duty as an offering to the Lord and receive the outcome as his blessing or *prasādam*. Then the results of his actions no longer have the ability to make his mind oscillate between agony and ecstasy. As his mind becomes more and more stable, he attains mastery over it and becomes ready for meditation. This is the way for beginners."

Establishing ourselves in meditation does not happen immediately for most of us. It is a process that depends on the state of our mind. Therefore Sri Krishna recommends selfless service as a mandatory activity for all those who want to meditate and realize the Self. The more we engage in *nishkāma Karma*, the more the mind is able to focus. Then meditation is a natural step forward.

If this is the process for a beginner with a scattered mind, what about a Yogi who has already mastered his mind? How does meditation work for him? It is true that a Yogi has mastery over his conscious mind. Most of his intentions have surfaced and come under his control. However, there are still some hidden impressions in his subconscious mind. He has to become aware of these and gain mastery over them.

The silence of meditation and patience help him to drop these impressions. Then he is ready to enter into the next phase of Yoga or higher state of consciousness.

Thus Sri Krishna defines how meditation should be approached by a beginner with a scattered mind and a Yogi who has mental mastery.

ārurukṣhor muner yogaṁ
Karma kāraṇam uchyate I
yogārūḍhasya tasyaiva
śhamaḥ kāraṇam uchyate II6.3II

****

Shloka 6.5

Elevate yourself through the power of your mind, and not degrade yourself, for the mind can be the friend and also the enemy of the Self

uddharet ātmanā, ātmānam - You have to uplift yourself with your mind (ātma means mind here). The mind is used to uplift oneself. The mind should not be allowed - *avasādayet* — to make for the downfall of yourself. Mind can uplift you, mind can be your downfall - should not allow your mind to cause your downfall. The mind itself - *bandhuḥ* - is your friend, and *ripuḥ* - your enemy.

Krishna beautifully tells the process of spiritual enlightenment, the upliftment. Mind is your vehicle, mind is an instrument. Just like your car, scooter, the mind is your vehicle, mind is not you. So use the vehicle for going to a specific destination. Use the vehicle to go to a place, where you want to go. What happens if you use a vehicle without a brake? You will be in trouble, you will meet with an accident. Mind is such an intelligent vehicle, the steering wheel of the mind and the brake of the mind should be under your control. Otherwise the vehicle called mind can take you anywhere. It can help you to go to a destination which you want or it will make you fall. It can uplift you or it can cause your downfall. So mastery of the mind is very important.

We think that we have friends and enemies. Enemy is one who hurts us. Friend is one who brings joy to us. Let's say, one of your enemies hurt you a few years ago. But that hurt is fresh in your mind, anytime. Everytime you remember that person, you get hurt. The person is no longer there but the hurt is there in your mind. So who is causing you the hurt, not the enemy, but your mind. Mind is constantly bringing up the memory and causing you pain. So who is your real enemy? It is your mind. Not the other person.

Who is a friend? Meeting a friend brings us joy. But the friend goes away. Nevertheless, remembering the friend makes you feel joyful. Where is the joy coming from? It is coming from the mind. So, who is your real friend? Mind.

Mind is both the enemy and friend. Mind is a vehicle. Handle that vehicle very carefully. Drive that vehicle very carefully. So a real spiritual sādhana is mastery over the mind. In India, we call people as great warriors or Mahaveera, not a person who has killed many people, not a person who has conquered kingdom, but one who has conquered his mind, one who has become free from mental delusions, the mental defilements like anger, jealousy and all those things is called a Mahaveera or Great Warrior. The one who has conquered the internal enemy is called the Mahaveera. Similarly the Buddhist call such a person as Arihanta. One who has conquered the internal enemy is called Arihanta. So Sri Krishna is advising Arjuna: learn to conquer your mind, learn to master your mind, because the mind itself causes your upliftment or downfall. Handle the vehicle called mind very carefully.

uddhared ātmanātmānaṁ
nātmānam avasādayet I
ātmaiva hyātmano bandhur

ātmaiva ripurātmanaḥ II6.5II

****

Shloka 6.10

Those who seek the state of Yoga should reside in seclusion, constantly engaged in meditation with a controlled mind and body, getting rid of desires and possessions for enjoyment

Yogi yuñjīta satatam ātmānaṁ rahasi sthitaḥ - a Yogi has to stay in a secluded place, a secret place for meditating on the Self. He should have *yata-chittātmā* - the mind and body mastered; *nirāśhīh* - without attachment; *aparigrahaḥ* - not expecting anything. Yogi has to stay in a place for meditation. Sri Krishna gives instructions for meditation practice. Where should you meditate?

You should meditate in a secluded place, a secret place. Why a secluded place? The place where you would have less distraction from the people or surroundings. In today's world, there are many distractions: the mobile phone, the television, the friends, the politics, the news, so many things can distract you. For mediation you need to have a focused mind. Forget about meditation, suppose a student wants to secure very good marks in an examination, what does he do? He will lock himself in a room, he will not hook onto the television, the internet, the mobile phone; locks himself in a room, a secluded place, where he has less distractions and starts studying. Whether it is for study or meditation, you need a secluded place where you have less distractions from people. This is very important. The place has to be secluded to the extent possible. The idea is to avoid distraction.

Next the mind and body have to be mastered. The mind and the body are the vehicles for spiritual practices. The body and the mind are the temple of the divine. So the body and mind have to be kept in a good condition for meditation. If the body gives trouble then meditation becomes difficult. So the mind also has to be calm. For the calmness of the mind you should be nirāśhīḥ, which means not attached to anything, not expecting anything. So all attachments have to be dropped, all attachments to food, achievement, success, name, fame have to be dropped; because otherwise the mind will crave out for that.

So you may wonder how it's possible to drop all the attachments? It is possible when you aim for the higher. A person who runs Olympics, aims for an Olympics medal, will spend years in training, will not get into movies, he will not get into any distractions by any other practices, nor gets distracted by friends. He will keep on focusing on his practice, in the view of winning the Olympics medal. A student who wants to get very good marks in the examination will not be distracted by anything. So similarly a person who is aspiring for the highest achievement in life which is enlightenment, which is God realization, will focus on meditation and Self Realization without getting attached to anything in life, a very natural process, a very simple process. Bhagavān is outlining that here.

Yogi yuñjīta satatam ātmānaṁ rahasi sthitaḥ I
ekākī yata-chittātmā nirāśhīr aparigrahaḥ II6.10II

****

Shloka 6.15

Thus, constantly keeping the mind absorbed in Me, the Yogi of disciplined mind attains nirvāṇ, and abides in Me in supreme peace

yuñjann evaṁ sadātmānaṁ - while meditating, the mind has to be engaged continuously, *niyata-mānasaḥ* - and controlled. Then, *mat-sansthām paramāṁ adhigachchhati* - one can attain to that the supreme bliss which is there in Me, says Sri Krishna.

So Sri Krishna gives here the *phala* or the result of meditation. What do I get by meditation? A student studies well with the intention of getting good marks, so that he can get a good job. He has focus, if he has to get a good job he has to study well. Similarly when we meditate what should be the focus?

The result of meditation, says Sri Krishna, is supreme bliss, ultimate bliss, the bliss of the inner Self, *ātma*. For that the Yogi has to continue his practice unwaveringly to establish his mind in the inner Self. We have the concept that meditation is for calming the mind, for getting different experiences, subtle experiences… Yes, all those things will happen in meditation, some light will be there, some sound, some vision, but these are all normal in the practice of meditation.

The purpose of meditation however is to go beyond the subtle sound and visions and establish in the supreme bliss in your own Self, in your own inner nature. Many people get distracted depending on the experience they have in meditation. The Yogi attains the ultimate supreme bliss when he does not lose focus. After attaining that state, the Yogi will not hanker for anything else, because the lesser, smaller joys of meditation will cease to matter.

yuñjann evaṁ sadātmānaṁ
Yogi niyata-mānasaḥ I
śhāntiṁ nirvāṇa-paramāṁ
mat-sansthām adhigachchhati II6.15II

****

Shloka 6.17

***But those who are temperate in eating and
recreation, balanced in work, and regulated in
sleep, can mitigate all sorrows by practicing Yoga***
yogo bhavati duḥkha-hā - the Yoga which removes all
suffering, duhkha is suffering, *duhkha-ha* is that
which removes suffering. Such a Yoga that removes
all suffering can be attained by one who is engaged
in meditation practices, but conditions apply!
yuktāhāra - the right kind of food has to be taken,
vihāra - the right kind of recreation, *yukta-cheṣhṭasya
Karmasu* - the effort has to be moderate;
yukta-svapnāvabodhasya - the right amount of
sleeping and waking hours are also important for
Yoga.

Sri Krishna tells us that moderation in life is very
important. When Gautama Siddharta started
practicing meditation, he undertook intense tapasya
for enlightenment, liberation. He went to the forest to
meditate and understood that the body is the cause

of suffering. So he stopped eating food, and his body became very weak, incapable of any physical activity. Then Siddhartha spotted a musician playing the Veena, a musical instrument, and it suddenly dawned on him that if the strings of the instrument are very tight, they will break, if the strings are very loose then no music will come. For beautiful music to emerge there should be moderate tension in the strings. That's when Siddhartha decided to tone down his extreme practices to moderate levels.

This is what Sri Krishna tells Arjuna, tells us, do not go to extremes, practice moderation in all walks of life; if you sleep too much you will be lazy, if you sleep too little you will fall asleep during meditation. The right kind of food has to be taken- *āhāra*. What is the right kind of food? The food which is satvik in nature, food that gives you energy and doesn't cause tamas- puts you to sleep. *vihāra* - even in exercise and recreation, undertake some amount of exercise so that the body is fit.

Meditation is not something which you can do by extreme effort; it's like sleep- the harder one tries to sleep, the more difficult it is. One simply falls asleep when there is no effort involved. Meditation is also a 'happening'. It happens spontaneously when the right effort is put with an attitude of surrender, as prescribed by Sri Krishna.

yuktāhāra-vihārasya yukta-cheṣhṭasya Karmasu I
yukta-svapnāvabodhasya yogo bhavati duḥkha-hā
II6.17II

****

Shloka 6.41

The unsuccessful Yogis, upon death, go to the subtle realm where the virtuous dwell. After dwelling there for a very long time, they are reborn on earth in a family of pious, prosperous people

In the 40th shloka, Arjuna asks Sri Krishna an intriguing question, "What happens to a Yogi who has performed *sādhana* but failed to attain liberation by the time he dies? Does all the effort that he has put in go waste?" Why did Arjuna ask this question? Sri Krishna is giving him divine wisdom and at the same time telling him to fight the war to protect Dharma. Arjuna has not yet attained liberation, but he may die on the war field while fighting. That is why he is worried.   Sri Krishna replies to this question in the 41st shloka. What does he say?

He calls such a Yogi a *yoga bhrashta*.   To understand the context, we can look at an example. Let us say that a student has studied very well for an exam. Unfortunately for various reasons, he is unable to attend the exam. What happens to him? He gets an opportunity to use this knowledge in the supplementary exam and score high marks. The *yoga bhrashta* is also in a similar position.

Sri Krishna says, "If a Yogi performs even a small amount of sadhana before he dies, he will certainly benefit from it in his next life. None of his effort is wasted. As soon as he dies, his good merit takes him to heavenly realms to experience many kinds of pleasure. When his merit is exhausted, he is reborn on earth. The family in which he is reborn is pious and prosperous. So he can focus on his sadhana. He continues his spiritual practices from the point where death interrupted them in his previous lifetime. There is nothing called failure in Yoga. Whether the Yogi is walking on the path of Karma Yoga, Bhakti Yoga or Jnāna Yoga in this life, it will continue in his next one. He will be reborn in a family of righteous people where he learns good values. If we learn the right way of thinking and living during childhood, it nurtures good samskaras or impressions in us which help us to realize the Self. Yes, it is easy to understand this. But why should he be born in a rich family? How is that helpful in his spiritual growth? In our childhood we enjoy the pleasures that money can buy. In a while we understand that the happiness they bring is always temporary and therefore worthless. So we begin to seek something higher.

This happened to Bhagavān Buddha. As we know, he was born in a royal family. He was a prince and could have anything he wished, but he soon tired of this and sought enlightenment instead. Sri Ramana Maharshi is another example. He was born in a dharmic family to spiritual parents. His upbringing helped him to attain liberation.

That is why Sri Krishna assures Arjuna, "Don't worry. Whatever you have practiced and learnt in this life will come to your aid in your next one even if you do not survive in this battle. You will continue your sadhana from wherever it gets broken off now. You will progress relentlessly on the spiritual path till you attain liberation."

*prāpya puṇya-kṛitāṁ lokān
uṣhitvā śhāśhvatīḥ samāḥ I
śhuchīnāṁ Srimatāṁ gehe
yoga-bhraṣhṭo 'bhijāyate II6.41II*

****

Shloka 6.47

Of all Yogis, those whose minds are always absorbed in Me, and who engage in devotion to Me with great faith, them I consider to be the highest of all

Yoginām api sarveshāṁ - of all the Yogis, *mad-gatenāntar-ātmanā* - the one with a single-pointed mind for realizing Me, which is God, Bhagavān, *shraddhāvān bhajate yo māṁ* - one who is putting effort towards that with faith, *sa me yukta tamah* - he is supreme, he is greater (than other Yogis).

Sri Krishna Bhagavān earlier spoke of different types of Yogis - a Karma Yogi, a *Jnāna-Karma-Sanyāsa Yogi, Karma-Sanyāsa Yogi.* So Yogis are of several types - Bhakti Yogi, people who worship the Lord in different ways. Of all these Yogis, one who has unwavering faith in Bhagavān, one who is constantly focusing on realizing the Supreme Lord in his heart, in his antar-atma, he is superior.

In any area of life, there will always be a lot of people putting in some effort to realize (their goal. For example in the area of sports, there are people who run the race at district level, some at state level, some at street level, and there are people who run the race at national level. There are people who focus on winning the Olympic gold medal and they focus very hard. They have faith in themselves, and they focus with single-minded focus on the Olympics. Similarly there are many Yogis. They practice Yoga, different kinds of Yoga. There are very few Yogis who have total faith in realizing God as their inner reality. Such Yogis put constant effort to realize Me, which is Bhagavān, the in-dweller of all beings. He is the greatest. That is the message of Bhagavān.

Yoginām api sarveṣhāṁ
mad-gatenāntar-ātmanā I
śhraddhāvān bhajate yo māṁ
sa me yuktatamo mataḥ II 6.47 II

Om Sadgurudevaya Namaha

PURCHASE DETAILS

(Scan QR codes to visit these links)

Book Purchase: https://notionpress.com/author/592662

CONTACT DETAILS

(Scan QR codes to visit these links)

Website: www.lightoftheself.org

Programs from Light of the SELF Foundation

1. **Atma Darshana** - Journey of Self discovery

2. **Jnāna Jyothi** - Study Advaita Vedanta

3. **Gita Jyoti** - Study Bhagavad Gita

4. **Yuva Jyoti** - iLeader Youth Leadership Program

5. **Bhakti Jyoti** - Learn Veda Mantras and Bhajans

6. **Yoga Jyoti** - Learn Yoga

Email id : lightofself@gmail.com